Dover, Delaware: Historical Guide for Travelers

American Cities History Guidebook Series

Henry Church

Published by Fiel LLC, 2023.

While every precaution has been taken in the preparation of this book, the publisher assumes no responsibility for errors or omissions, or for damages resulting from the use of the information contained herein.

DOVER, DELAWARE: HISTORICAL GUIDE FOR TRAVELERS

First edition. September 19, 2023.

Copyright © 2023 Henry Church.

ISBN: 979-8223887720

Written by Henry Church.

Also by Henry Church

American Cities History Guidebook Series
Charlottesville, Virginia: Historical Guide for Travelers
Williamsburg, Virginia: Historical Guide for Travelers
Richmond, Virginia: Historical Guide for Travelers
Norfolk & Virginia Beach: Historical Guide for Travelers
Winchester, Virginia: Historical Guide for Travelers
Baltimore, Maryland: Historical Guide for Travelers
Dover, Delaware: Historical Guide for Travelers
Arlington, Virginia: Historical Guide for Travelers

Table of Contents

Introduction

Imagine yourself opening these pages and stepping into the soil of Dover, Delaware, where each grain of sand seems to be carrying a whisper of the events and people that have molded not only this city but the entire country. This is a land that has seen European explorers cross the Delaware River in search of new lands to colonize, heard the ferocious speeches of revolutionaries rallying their followers to fight against British rule, and seen the soaring triumphs and sobering difficulties that make the American story so compelling. Dover is a character, a real, breathing being with lessons to impart and tales to tell. It is not only a background.

The process of learning about Dover's history is similar to putting together a challenging jigsaw; each piece, whether it is a pivotal conflict, a significant local, or a game-changing law, carries a distinct meaning. But the complete picture only becomes apparent when these parts interact. We'll start by going through Dover's history, which has its roots in the Delaware Colony, and then look at how it came to be a key location during the American Revolution. We'll examine the architecture that has shaped its identity, from colonial-era structures to contemporary constructions, and learn about the famous and unknown people that have traversed its streets. Names like Caesar Rodney, a Continental Congress delegate and person enshrined in bronze at Rodney Square, will come to life when placed in the context of a city and era vastly apart from our own.

This journey, however, won't just go from the past to the present; it will jump around in time to demonstrate how the echoes of Dover's history are still felt in the city's modern cultural, economic, and social landscapes. From being a peaceful colonial colony to becoming the state capital of Delaware with a diverse range of industry and educational institutions, the town has seen major changes. The Dover International Speedway, Dover Air Force Base, and Delaware State University are just a few of the contemporary sites we'll talk about in relation to their historical significance and present-day significance.

But without its inhabitants, what is a city? We'll explore the communities that have thrived here, from Native Americans to European settlers, from African Americans who fought for civil rights to immigrants who added to Dover's rich tapestry of diversity. We'll delve into the subcultures that make Dover special. These groups have played a significant role in establishing the identity of the city, participating in social movements, influencing policy, and even innovating in the field of technology.

We will carefully connect the past with the present as we explore Dover's history and discuss how historical individuals and events have shaped the city we live in today. Knowing Dover's past can help you navigate its future, whether you're addressing environmental issues, the city's economic prospects, or ongoing discussions about equity and justice.

Therefore, this book strives to be your informed travel companion whether you're a native looking for a closer connection to your ancestors, a visitor eager to discover an American historical gem, or someone hoping to grasp the many facets of Dover. Let's set out on this historical exploration and unearth the many layers of history that have contributed to Dover, Delaware's status as a national treasure full of untold tales and priceless teachings.

Chapter 1: Native Tribes of Dover

Dover was home to indigenous peoples who had a close and long-lasting relationship with the land before European explorers marked their way across the Delaware River, before the colonies started to form a new world, and long before the American Revolution redefined freedom. The foundational layer of Dover's intricate tapestry is made up of their history, which is frequently overlooked by the inflow of later settlements and the tidal waves of cultural development. This chapter tries to give light on the cultures, social systems, and environmental knowledge that shaped the manner of life of the Native American tribes that previously called Dover home.

Tribes like the Lenape (also known as the Delaware Indians) and the Nanticoke once lived on the region that Dover now occupies. These tribes belonged to the greater Algonquian linguistic group, and their societies were intricately structured and firmly established in cultural practices that emphasized the interdependence of people and the natural world. For instance, the Lenape were skilled in agriculture, fishing, and hunting. They grew crops including maize, beans, and squash, which are frequently referred to as the "Three Sisters" due to their complementing growing habits. These tribes viewed themselves as essential elements of an ecological equilibrium rather than as being distinct from the environment.

These tribes practiced matrilineal society, in which inheritance and lineage were passed down through the mother's side. The tribes' profound respect for the earth—often personified as a feminine entity—was reflected in their social system. Men and women both held important responsibilities in society and religion; gender roles did exist but they were flexible. The tribes' religious practices placed a strong emphasis on a cosmology in which spirits lived in a variety of elements of the natural world, whether in creatures, plants, or celestial bodies. These spirits controlled the course of the seasons, the amount of wildlife, and the prosperity of harvests. They were not only inert forces.

The indigenous inhabitants of Dover had intricate systems of government, with chieftains being chosen for their sagacity, bravery, or spiritual understanding. These chiefs, whether they were men or women, guided their tribes in council, took part in diplomacy, and, regrettably, occasionally had to get into battle. Alliances between tribes were prevalent, and they were formed for a variety of reasons, such as trade, defense, and marriage. Pottery, textiles, and weaponry were frequently traded, but it was probably the knowledge—farming methods, navigational routes, and medical formulas—that was passed down from one generation to the next that was most valuable.

Sadly, the beginning of European colonization resulted in terrible changes for Dover's native population. Because they lacked innate protection, diseases like smallpox decimated communities. Conflicts resulted from territorial invasions, and the entrance of the Europeans greatly damaged the natural resources that the Indians relied on. Many were evicted from their ancestral estates or forced into servitude. However, this story is not just one of victimization. The Lenape and Nanticoke actively negotiated with European settlers, and their descendants continued to have a significant impact on Delaware's history by acting as interpreters and guides and taking part in court decisions that reshaped land rights.

Dover's indigenous history is now commemorated in a number of ways, including educational initiatives, museums, and heritage events. Furthermore, it is critical to acknowledge and honor the contributions that current members of these tribes continue to make to Dover and the larger American community. The unmistakable takeaway from this chapter is that the Native tribes of Dover were complex communities with profound beliefs and intricate lifestyles, not just forerunners to subsequent developments. Understanding their legacy is essential for understanding not only the entirety of Dover's history, but also the ecological and social insights that may be invaluable in resolving today's and tomorrow's difficulties.

In the next chapters, we'll examine how Dover evolved from an indigenous region into a colonial settlement, assuming several identities over time. But as we proceed, let's not forget the original inhabitants of this territory, whose deeds and legacies served as the foundation for the metropolis.

Chapter 2: Early Settlers and Their Stories

Dover was home to indigenous peoples who had a close and long-lasting relationship with the land before European explorers marked their way across the Delaware River, before the colonies started to form a new world, and long before the American Revolution redefined freedom. The foundational layer of Dover's intricate tapestry is made up of their history, which is frequently overlooked by the inflow of later settlements and the tidal waves of cultural development. This chapter tries to give light on the cultures, social systems, and environmental knowledge that shaped the manner of life of the Native American tribes that previously called Dover home.

Tribes like the Lenape (also known as the Delaware Indians) and the Nanticoke once lived on the region that Dover now occupies. These tribes belonged to the greater Algonquian linguistic group, and their societies were intricately structured and firmly established in cultural practices that emphasized the interdependence of people and the natural world. For instance, the Lenape were skilled in agriculture, fishing, and hunting. They grew crops including maize, beans, and squash, which are frequently referred to as the "Three Sisters" due to their complementing growing habits. These tribes viewed themselves as essential elements of an ecological equilibrium rather than as being distinct from the environment.

These tribes practiced matrilineal society, in which inheritance and lineage were passed down through the mother's side. The tribes' profound respect for the earth—often personified as a feminine entity—was reflected in their social system. Men and women both held important responsibilities in society and religion; gender roles did exist but they were flexible. The tribes' religious practices placed a strong emphasis on a cosmology in which spirits lived in a variety of elements of the natural world, whether in creatures, plants, or celestial bodies. These spirits controlled the course of the seasons, the amount of wildlife, and the prosperity of harvests. They were not only inert forces.

The indigenous inhabitants of Dover had intricate systems of government, with chieftains being chosen for their sagacity, bravery, or spiritual understanding. These chiefs, whether they were men or women, guided their tribes in council, took part in diplomacy, and, regrettably, occasionally had to get into battle. Alliances between tribes were prevalent, and they were formed for a variety of reasons, such as trade, defense, and marriage. Pottery, textiles, and weaponry were frequently traded, but it was probably the knowledge—farming methods, navigational routes, and medical formulas—that was passed down from one generation to the next that was most valuable.

Sadly, the beginning of European colonization resulted in terrible changes for Dover's native population. Because they lacked innate protection, diseases like smallpox decimated communities. Conflicts resulted from territorial invasions, and the entrance of the Europeans greatly damaged the natural resources that the Indians relied on. Many were evicted from their ancestral estates or forced into servitude. However, this story is not just one of victimization. The Lenape and

Nanticoke actively negotiated with European settlers, and their descendants continued to have a significant impact on Delaware's history by acting as interpreters and guides and taking part in court decisions that reshaped land rights.

Dover's indigenous history is now commemorated in a number of ways, including educational initiatives, museums, and heritage events. Furthermore, it is critical to acknowledge and honor the contributions that current members of these tribes continue to make to Dover and the larger American community. The unmistakable takeaway from this chapter is that the Native tribes of Dover were complex communities with profound beliefs and intricate lifestyles, not just forerunners to subsequent developments. Understanding their legacy is essential for understanding not only the entirety of Dover's history, but also the ecological and social insights that may be invaluable in resolving today's and tomorrow's difficulties.

In the next chapters, we'll examine how Dover evolved from an indigenous region into a colonial settlement, assuming several identities over time. But as we proceed, let's not forget the original inhabitants of this territory, whose deeds and legacies served as the foundation for the metropolis.

Chapter 3: Dover in the Colonial Era

Dover changed from a frontier town to a thriving colonial center in the 18th century, echoing greater changes that swept over America during this revolutionary time. Politics, trade, social complexity, and an intellectual upheaval that would lead to revolution are all abundant during this time. Dover was more than just a passive observer of these events; it was a microcosm of colonial America where the overarching issues of the time found dramatic local expression.

By the early 1700s, Dover had established itself as a key player in Delaware's economy and, consequently, that of the American colonies. The town developed into a hub of business thanks to its advantageous location along the St. Jones River. Local traders sent out tobacco, cereals, and timber in exchange for the products that trading ships brought in from Europe and the Caribbean. The activity at the Riverside mills was humming, turning local grain into flour for both nearby villages and far-off markets.

Dover was a melting pot of cultures and religions on a social level. In this time, where Calvinist principles and Enlightenment ideas collided, both social and political gatherings took place in bars. Although the town had at this point developed into a mosaic of religious connections, including Anglicans, Methodists, and Presbyterians, William

Penn's Quaker ideas still loomed large. Churches like Christ Church, which was founded in 1734, formed important parts of local culture and served as centers for both civic involvement and spiritual uplift.

Dover's history also includes the institution of slavery, which was tragically woven into the fabric of colonial society. Slaves labored in the fields and in people's houses, boosting the economy while also creating ethical dilemmas. Dover was a place where free Black people lived and made valuable contributions to society while negotiating the complicated terrain of racial relations. Their experiences, which are frequently underreported, shed light on how free Black Americans built dignified lives despite structural inequity.

Dover found itself at a turning point in history as hostilities between Britain and the American colonies grew more intense. Caesar Rodney, a patriotic native son, personified the revolutionary spirit of the community. His extraordinary journey to Philadelphia to cast Delaware's tie-breaking vote for independence from the United States is enshrined in the annals of American Revolutionary mythology. However, John Dickinson, a fellow Dover native and the author of the well-known "Letters from a Farmer in Pennsylvania," was not alone; he also made intellectual contributions to the revolutionary cause.

When Dover was chosen as the capital of Delaware in 1777, a strategic and symbolic move that reflected the state's growing prominence, the political excitement reached a peak. Its courts, town square, and pubs transformed became discussion forums for the ideas and doubts of a nation-in-formation. Politicians were not the only ones having these talks; common people also debated issues of government, liberty, and the future of the colonies in the marketplace, in churches, and at home.

In a ceremony held in Dover, Delaware became the first state to ratify the U.S. Constitution in 1787. It was a turning point in the city's development from a little trade post to a major intellectual and political hub. The ratification confirmed Dover's permanent position in the American constitutional system in addition to Delaware's statehood.

Despite the vast political themes, colonial Dover's daily life was a tapestry of commonplace yet significant events: farmers cultivating the land, artisans refining their craft, families attending church, and kids studying the alphabet in one-room schools. These routine activities served as the foundation for a neighborhood and, eventually, a country.

Thus, the Colonial Era is a key period in the history of Dover, laying the foundation for both exciting and difficult future growth. Dover had a significant role in the fabric of colonial life through its commercial endeavors, social intricacies, intellectual fervor, and political achievements. It was a site where the American dream's contradictions and potential were experienced and put to the test. As a result, it encourages us to reflect on not only what America became but also why and how it became so.

Chapter 4: Important Landmarks and their History

Each building, street, and monument in Dover is a silent testimony to a past that tells volumes about the city's rich history. In this chapter, we'll stroll through Dover's historic streets to look at the monuments that have withstood the test of time and capture the spirit of various periods in the city's growth.

The Green, Dover's historic center, should come first. The Green, which was built as a part of William Penn's original town plan, has been the site of numerous occasions that have influenced not only Dover but the entire country. Delaware became the first state to ratify the U.S. Constitution here in 1787. The Old State House, which was also finished in 1791, is one of the state government buildings that surround it today. It is a National Historic Landmark. A lesson in colonial aesthetics can be learned from the Old State House's Georgian architecture, which features finely carved woodwork and a distinctive cupola. The Old State House, which once housed the state's capitol, is now a museum that preserves historical artifacts such as discussions on legislation that shaped Delaware's early laws.

The John Dickinson Plantation, another important building nearby The Green, is situated nearby. John Dickinson, who is referred to as the "Penman of the Revolution" for his significant works, lived on this farm. The plantation provides a window into the agricultural sector, which was crucial to Delaware's colonial and post-colonial existence. Due to the fact that it was labored on by both free and enslaved labor, it also serves as a complicated emblem of early socioeconomic hierarchy in America. One can practically hear the echoes of the political and intellectual discussions that helped to develop revolutionary ideology in its rooms.

The Dover Air Force Base is a must-see tourist attraction for anyone with an interest in military history. The base, which was initially built during World War II as a municipal airfield, later developed into a key military facility and is now home to the Air Mobility Command Museum. The museum houses a remarkable collection of antique military aircraft and provides background information on America's role in many battles through aviation. The facility represents the history of Dover in the 20th century, but it also contributes to a larger story about American military and technical accomplishments.

The Delaware Agricultural Museum and Village, a facility devoted to preserving the state's agricultural past, serves as a home for cultural history. Everything from old farming tools to meticulously recreated rural dwellings can be found here, offering you a hands-on understanding of the agricultural practices that supported families and fuelled economies. The museum serves as a poignant reminder of Dover's roots in the productive fields of Delaware, even though it may not be as big as some other sites.

We should highlight the Schwartz Center for the Arts as we explore Dover's architectural landscape. Although the structure has gone through phases of closure and reconstruction, its historical significance as a hub for arts and culture in the neighborhood cannot be emphasized. The Schwartz Center, which was initially constructed as an opera theatre in the early 1900s, has since held everything from vaudeville events to contemporary musical performances, reflecting America's changing cultural preferences over the years.

Christ Episcopal Church is distinctive in Dover's religious landscape. This historic structure, built in 1734, has witnessed Dover's development from a colonial settlement to a contemporary city. The building itself is a study in colonial religious aesthetics, and the church cemetery, where some of Dover's most important residents are buried, provides a serene setting for contemplating the complex history of the neighborhood.

The Delaware Legislative Hall, the location of the General Assembly in Delaware, is our final stop. This 1933-built Georgian Revival building represents the development of Dover as a major administrative hub. Legislative Hall, with its elaborate chambers and historical exhibits, is a functioning government facility as well as a functioning museum.

Dover is a true open-air museum where history is preserved through the city's buildings, open spaces, and other landmarks in addition to books and recollections. Each landmark acts as a lens, allowing us to see specific aspects of Dover's complicated past. They allow us to experience history firsthand by touching it and living it, so that we can see Dover not just as a city of the present but also as a series of richly different and colorful yesterdays.

Chapter 5: Dover during the American Revolution

Dover was caught up in the American colonies' revolutionary fever as the 1770s got underway. The ripples of opposition to British rule that had first been whispers became a tide that swept through homes, churches, and taverns. The concepts of liberty, representation, and independence found receptive ground in Dover, a town already entrenched in democratic rule and Enlightenment thought. In order to fully understand Dover's involvement in the American Revolution, this chapter will examine both its contributions on and off the battlefield as well as how the war affected the community at all levels.

Without mentioning Caesar Rodney, a politician whose dramatic journey to Philadelphia at midnight in 1776 clinched Delaware's vote for independence, any discussion of Dover's role in the Revolution would be incomplete. Rodney, who was born close to Dover and held a number of official positions, including Kent County Sheriff, was afflicted with a type of facial cancer and asthma at the time. Nevertheless, he traveled almost 80 miles through muddy tracks after mounting his horse in a deluge to break an impasse in the Delaware delegation at the Continental Congress. His vote served as a rallying cry, not merely for independence but also for Dover's revolutionary spirit. Later, Rodney would hold the office of President of Delaware, basically acting as the state's head of government. Under his guidance, the state was successfully navigated through the tumultuous war years.

However, Rodney wasn't the only Doveite to make a lasting impact. The renowned "Letters from a Farmer in Pennsylvania," written by John Dickinson, known as the "Penman of the Revolution," were instrumental in influencing public opinion against the Stamp Act and other British taxes without representation. Dickinson was a moderate who first attempted to mend relations with Britain, but his intellectual contributions helped lay the foundation for revolution.

Delaware's soldiers, notably those from Dover, developed a reputation for their bravery and tenacity on the battlefield. They were frequently known to as the "Delaware Blues" because of their distinctive blue uniforms that stood out in a sea of different colonial clothing. The regiment participated in a number of significant engagements, such as Long Island, White Plains, and Germantown. These guys had to contend with disease, insufficient food, and harsh winters in addition to the adversary they encountered on the battlefield.

The war had both immediate and long-term effects in Dover. British blockades hindered trade, which had an impact on local farmers and merchants who could no longer easily export their commodities. Families with men serving in the front experienced problems at home as taxes increased to fund the war effort. But the neighborhood also came together in inspiring ways. In addition to managing farms and enterprises, women participated in the war effort in a variety of ways, such as by sewing uniforms or caring for the injured. The community developed become a center for cutting-edge communication. Somewhat locally printed newspapers and pamphlets disseminated news and propaganda, fanning the flames of revolution and informing the public.

The churches in Dover also had an impact. More and more sermons adopted a revolutionary attitude, frequently using biblical stories to support the independence movement. Pastors and worshippers alike struggled with the ethical ramifications of rebellion and the intellectual foundations of a new nation, blurring the distinction between spiritual and temporal issues in these places of worship.

When the war was finally finished, Dover experienced a variety of effects. In terms of the economy, the town struggled to recover its trade and manage its wartime debts. Socially, the experience served as both a crucible and a catalyst, helping to define the American identity while also exposing problems like slavery that would persist as a source of tension for the country. Politically, the conflict cemented Dover's status as the seat of government for the young state of Delaware and the location where its new laws would be drafted.

However, psychological effects might have had the longest-lasting effects. The people of Dover came out of the Revolution with a stronger feeling of their own agency, a conviction that was firmly grounded in the knowledge that they had contributed, whether with their words, their voices, or their muskets, to the formation of a nation. The Revolution was a time in the town's history when ordinary people were caught up in the flow of significant historical events. It had been both a communal activity and a deeply personal one. Dover actively helped deliver the Revolution by participating in it, therefore it had not only seen the birth of a nation. And in doing so, it had permanently braided the spirit of revolution into the very foundation of its neighborhood, leaving a legacy that would reverberate for decades to come.

Chapter 6: Local Heroes and Events of Note

The history of a location isn't just based on seismic activity or well-known landmarks, as any historian or history enthusiast would attest. Sometimes the most vivid hues in a community's history palette come from local figures and lesser-known occasions. There is no exception to this in Dover, Delaware. While it has undoubtedly produced its fair share of notable figures and momentous events, a closer examination of its local heroes and noteworthy incidents reveals a richer, more complex fabric of human striving, adversity, and victory.

Consider the remarkable life of Annie Jump Cannon, who was born in Dover in 1863. Cannon, an astronomer whose research established the principles of modern stellar classification, encountered many challenges as a deaf woman working in a male-dominated field. She persisted in spite of this, cataloging over 350,000 stars over the course of a career that lasted more than 40 years while also earning various prizes and honorary degrees. Her biography, which is frequently overlooked by larger historical storylines, provides a compelling illustration of individual determination and genius coming from a little Delaware village and resonates as a timeless emblem of what can be accomplished despite the odds.

Similar to this, Dover native Dr. Muriel E. Gilman's life serves as an example of the pinnacle of volunteerism. Dr. Gilman played a crucial role in the expansion and modernization of Dover in the late 20th century. He was involved in a wide range of regional projects, including educational efforts and healthcare improvements. She is affectionately remembered as one of the town's most effective and charitable leaders, despite the fact that her efforts may not have received as much attention as those of political or military officials.

Another local matter that merits consideration is Dover's role in the Underground Railroad. The village itself wasn't a big center, but it was an essential part of the underground system that allowed slaves to escape and find freedom. Black and white local abolitionists put their lives and freedom at risk to help with this dangerous voyage north. One of them was Thomas Garrett, a Quaker who was active in Delaware but was born in Upper Darby, Pennsylvania. Thomas Garrett openly disobeyed the laws of his era to aid those seeking independence. His associations with Harriet Tubman have received extensive coverage. These unique acts of bravery and kindness not only touched the lives of numerous people, but they also quietly changed the social and moral climate of Dover, adding complexity to the story of that city's past.

Don't forget the Dover Days Festival, a noteworthy occasion that began in 1933 as a tiny garden party. What was once a small gathering has grown into an annual event honoring Dover's history that draws tens of thousands of people. The history of the town is brought to life in a collective celebration through historical recreations, parades, and customary crafts. The occasion creates a common setting for both reflection and celebration as the community looks back on and celebrates its own past.

Additionally, the Battle of Dover, a lesser-known battle during the War of 1812, is particularly remembered in the area. Even though it was not a major fight in the grand scheme of the war, the conflict inspired the local population and strengthened its militias. For residents of Dover, it was a moving example of their community's fragility as well as its resiliency and capacity to band together in the face of difficulty.

These are only a few of the innumerable individuals, occasions, and projects that have influenced Dover's history. These individuals—from educators and activists to scientists and everyday citizens—and their actions have all added threads to the complex history of Dover. Some made a lasting impression with large, overarching actions, while others did so through subtle, steadfast deeds that over time had an impact on the community's ethos.

While not all of them may be well-known on a national or even an international level, their influence extends far beyond the city limits of Dover. Future generations, who will inherit not only historical details and sites, but also the spirit of innovation, service, and community that these local heroes and events exemplify, can draw inspiration from their stories. These stories provide us with both anchors and compasses as we travel through Dover's history, establishing us in the town's particular story and leading us toward a richer, more thorough understanding of what makes Dover, in all its complexity and nuance, a crucial chapter in the larger American story.

Chapter 7: Post-Revolution Changes and Development

Dover found itself negotiating a landscape of change and difficulty after the American Revolution as it evolved from a colonial outpost to a crucial component of a developing nation. The cessation of wars with Britain created new trade and development prospects, but it also raised issues with governance, social organization, and economic focus. This chapter dives into Dover's post-Revolutionary transformation, analyzing the variables that drove its development and highlighting the key events that helped to define its contemporary identity.

The problem of governance was among the immediate issues Dover had to deal with after the war. Delaware had enacted its first constitution in 1776, although there were discussions about changes and improvements in the years immediately after the Revolution. Dover, which had established itself as the state capital by the year 1777, became the focal point of these political debates. Due to the town's status as the capital, a large number of public officials, attorneys, and other professionals moved there to start up homes or businesses. This increased political activity sparked the construction of courthouses and legislative buildings, strengthening Dover's position as the center of Delaware's government.

The years following the Revolution were both optimistic and uncertain economically. On the one hand, the abandonment of British mercantilist policies gave Dover traders more leeway to investigate foreign markets. On the other hand, the economy had become shaky due to the loss of the British market and war-related expenses. But the growth of agriculture, notably the production of grains and fruits, gave the economy a much-needed boost. Dover benefited from these agricultural developments as it was located in a fertile area of the Delaware River Valley, making it a prime position for shipping commodities to bigger towns like Philadelphia and Baltimore.

In the years following the Revolution, the issue of slavery also predominated. Delaware was a slave-owning state, but things were starting to change. One of Dover's Revolutionary War heroes, Caesar Rodney, had owned slaves in the past. But his nephew Caesar A. Rodney would grow into a passionate opponent of slavery. Delaware was taking baby measures toward liberation during this time, but complete abolition wouldn't happen until the 13th Amendment was ratified in 1865. The arguments and disagreements surrounding this matter brought to light the complicated ideological and moral issues Dover had to deal with as it adapted to a new national and cultural environment.

Not only was the political and economic landscape altering, but also Dover's overall appearance. The colonial era's more straightforward, practical architectural advancements gave way to more elaborate designs influenced by European neoclassicism and the Federal style. These changes represented a broader cultural evolution and reflected the optimism of the young country as well as its determination to make its identity known on a global scale. Dover's outward appearance was altered during this time, but its social and cultural life was also enhanced by the construction of schools, churches, and public gathering places.

It's significant to note that numerous social and civic organizations expanded throughout this time. There were several literary societies, charitable organizations, and business associations that promoted intellectual exchange and social harmony. The social structure and intellectual atmosphere of the town were greatly influenced by these organizations, which helped to establish a culture that valued both individual initiative and group well-being.

Dover underwent significant change in the years following the Revolution. Dover was developing its identity at this time, one that combined its colonial past with its emerging national ethos, amid the whirlwind of political arguments, economic ups and downs, and social transformation. It involved learning to strike a balance between the liberties achieved during the Revolution and the demands of governance, the promises of economic opportunity with the difficulties presented by a changing economy, and the lofty ideals of a new nation with the intricate reality of its social fabric.

Through it all, Dover emerged as a town that had not only survived a revolution but also learned its wonderful and bitter lessons. The town's post-Revolutionary evolution was a microcosm of a country coping with the realities and ambiguities of its newfound independence, reflecting the larger upheavals sweeping through the young United States. We learn more about Dover's special place in American history—and possibly about America itself—by analyzing this complex dance between the past and present, ideal and reality.

Chapter 8: Industry and Infrastructure Growth

The story of Dover's industrial and infrastructure growth is not just one of bricks, mortar, and machines; it is also one of human aspiration, invention, and community development. The transformation of Dover from a community with a predominately agrarian economy into one that embraced industrialization is a multi-layered narrative that highlights the town's and its residents' entrepreneurial spirit against the backdrop of America's industrial period.

Dover experienced a transition from an agrarian economic model to one that included a variety of emerging sectors as the 19th century went on. Although Delaware's rich soil continued to support a thriving agricultural industry, the economic landscape was expanding in new directions. The St. Jones River's banks were dotted by mills that processed cereals, timber, and textiles by the mid-1800s. These mills, which were frequently family-run enterprises, laid the groundwork for a more diverse economy by offering both goods and employment possibilities.

The Delaware Railroad's arrival in Dover in 1855 was among the most significant developments for the city's infrastructure and business sector. This rail connection served as a commercial thoroughfare, enabling commodities to be transported more swiftly and affordably, opening up previously closed markets. Notably, Dover became the terminus of the Delaware Railroad, giving the city more economic significance.

It is difficult to overestimate the railroad's contribution to Dover's development. It not only sped up industrial growth, but it also made space for important infrastructure developments like better roads and bridges, which drew in additional settlers and investors.

The beginning of Dover's manufacturing age was in the late 19th and early 20th century. Carriage, paper, and machinery manufacturing plants started to spring up. The J. Caleb Boggs Hosiery Mill, one of the biggest knitting mills in the state, was a prominent establishment. Not only did it help the economy, but it also fundamentally altered Dover's social structure. The town saw an inflow of immigrants and workers from all regions of the country as manufacturers needed a larger workforce. Each brought their own cultural influences and shaped Dover's more multicultural character.

Infrastructure expanded at a similar rate as the industrial sector. Dover's waterworks and electrical infrastructure were built in direct response to the demands of a developing industrial sector. Similarly, Dover's public services, including its schools and hospitals, grew as more people moved there in search of employment. These infrastructure upgrades weren't just results of economic expansion; they were also calculated bets made to increase Dover's desirability to both businesses and residents, igniting a positive feedback loop of growth and development.

Dover's industrial and infrastructure history also has underlying social and labor history implications. Industrialization brought riches, but it also sparked debates over social injustice, salary disparities, and workers' rights. For example, the establishment of the International Ladies' Garment employees' Union local in Dover in 1919 shows how employees are becoming more organized and aware of the need to fight for improved working conditions and wages.

At the beginning of the century, Dover was also struggling with the problems of modernity. Horse-drawn carriages started to be replaced by automobiles, necessitating the construction of new roads and automotive services. The development of the Dover Air Force Base during World War II added yet another layer to the community's economic structure, injecting federal funds and generating jobs in industries like aviation technology and construction.

Looking back, it's clear that Dover's transformation from a small agricultural community to a major industrial center with a solid infrastructure wasn't predetermined. It was the outcome of numerous interrelated factors, including the creativity of its businesspeople, the fortitude of its employees, the foresight of its civic leaders, and the arc of wider economic and technical trends. Each period left its mark, each person added a verse, and together they created the intricate, dynamic tapestry that still defines Dover's economic and social environment.

We enter into a narrative replete with dreams, difficulties, disappointments, and victories in order to grasp Dover's industrial and infrastructural evolution rather than just following the outlines of buildings, roads, or industries. This tale, which captures the spirit of both the town and the country it calls home, offers priceless insights into how Dover managed the challenges and possibilities presented by a changing world to forge its own unique identity within the context of American history.

Chapter 9: Dover During the Civil War

Dover experienced a period of significant internal conflict during the Civil War, that great American crucible, which also affected the rest of the nation. Dover, which is located in a border state, was in an unusual and frequently perilous situation throughout this tumultuous time. Delaware was a microcosm of the tensions in the country with its northern industrial leanings and southern rural character. The state did not secede, but it also did not fully support the Union cause, particularly when it came to the slavery issue. This chapter aims to examine the social, economic, and political ramifications that followed as it examines how Dover, as a representative Delawarean community, traversed the minefield of national divisiveness throughout the Civil War years.

Dover's perspective on the war was complicated, braided with strands of pragmatism, ideological conflict, and allegiance. Dover had a fair amount of supporters of both the Union and the Confederacy even though Delaware remained a part of the Union. The town embodied the complexity and ambiguities of a border state and was a boiling pot of divergent viewpoints. As a reflection of the wider discussions taking place on the national stage, public meetings frequently turned into forums for contentious debate. Despite this ideological divide, the people of Dover shared a common concern about the war's effects on their neighborhood, with everyone from farmers to business owners experiencing the effects on the local economy.

Dover's economy was impacted by the war in a number of ways. Due to blockades and continued hostilities, prospective markets in the South were closed off, which had an impact on trade. The demand for agricultural products, particularly grains, was erratic. It was affected by the requirements of the Union forces as well as by labor market uncertainty because slavery was a divisive subject. Farms and businesses in the area were left understaffed because so many local men enrolled or were conscripted into military service. On the other hand, certain industrial activity was stimulated by the war economy, including the creation of textiles for military uniforms and the expansion of small companies serving the needs of service members and their families.

Particular attention should be paid to the African American community of Dover's contribution to the war effort. Dover, Delaware, was a slave state, and its residents were slaveholders as a rule. The war did, however, serve as a spur for reform. African American males may find freedom and a method to support the effort to end slavery by enlisting in the Union Army. Although Delaware didn't technically abolish slavery until the Thirteenth Amendment was ratified in 1865, the institution did diminish during the war. During and after the war, Dover's African American community started to assert itself more strongly, setting the framework for the subsequent civil rights movements.

Dover's political climate during the Civil War was tense. The town served as a hub for political activity because it was the state capital. Conscription, habeas corpus, and wartime taxation were some of the difficult issues that the Delaware legislature struggled with. The allegiances of influential Doverites were rigorously examined, and people frequently had to wade through intricate webs of allegiance. Delaware was a Union state, but the federal government was still keeping an eye on it because they were worried about any Confederate sympathies. A culture of distrust and caution was present due to the frequent accusations and denials of treason.

Dover's social structure and communal consciousness changing throughout the Civil War may be its most enduring legacies. The transformation was sped up by the war. Like the country as a whole, Dover came out of the Civil War with a greater awareness of its own complexity and paradoxes. In order to make room for new economic, social, and political paradigms, the previous order had been challenged and in some ways demolished.

We interact with a community at a crossroads, attempting to regain its footing in a world flipped upside down, as we learn about Dover during the Civil War. The struggles endured, decisions made, and lessons discovered throughout these turbulent years provide a window into the American psyche, demonstrating the frailty and resiliency of democratic principles in the face of unimaginable calamity. By using this perspective, the Civil War experience in Dover may be seen as both a particular local tale and a larger allegory for a country that is attempting to remake itself while grappling with internal tensions.

Chapter 10: Reconstruction and its Impact

Dover also found itself coping with the post-war reality when the Civil War's guns fell silent and the country started the difficult process of Reconstruction. This time period, frequently referred to as one of America's most complex, was one of adaptation and reinvention, characterized by complexity, paradoxes, and a great deal of introspection. The abolition of slavery and the emergence of newly empowered African Americans as participants in public life are two of the seismic transformations that Dover grappled with during Reconstruction.

Dover tried to put the spirit of the Reconstruction legislation into practice during this time, which resulted in substantial social and political instability. The Thirteenth, Fourteenth, and Fifteenth Amendments changed the legal landscape of the country by granting African Americans the rights to freedom, citizenship, and the ability to vote. Although these new amendments were ground-breaking in letter, their execution was the real test. And it was in this crucible of transition that Dover showed both its liberal leanings and its traditional conservatism.

The African American community in Dover actively participated in the rebuilding of their communities and way of life. To educate the newly emancipated people, schools were created. Institutions like the Union American Methodist Episcopal Church served as hubs for political and communal activism in addition to being spiritual havens. The dialogues taking place in Dover's public realm were frequently shaped by the church's pastors, who frequently played important roles as advocates for justice and civil rights.

Resistance, however, hampered the advancement. The emergence of white supremacist movements and beliefs was a reflection of the opposition to the advancements of the African American population. This conflict showed up in a variety of ways, sometimes as overtly antagonistic behavior and other times as structural impediments meant to maintain inequality. For example, despite the fact that African American men were given the right to vote, a number of voter suppression strategies, such as poll fees and literacy tests, were used to prevent them from engaging in politics. These problems were made worse by discriminatory policies in employment, housing, and education, which paved the way for the civil rights struggles of the 20th century.

After a conflict that upended its traditional rural way of life, Dover had to remake itself economically. The labor market had to be changed as a result of the abolition of slavery. In terms of economic independence, many former slaves now worked as tenant farmers or sharecroppers, which were frequently just marginally better than slavery. However, when the Delaware Railroad rebuilt connections with markets in both the North and South, the end of the war also heralded a boom in trade and a restoration of industrial prospects. The economic void presented a chance for a number of Dover's innovative residents, who engaged in new businesses, some of which would set the foundation for Dover's industrial profile in the 20th century.

During Reconstruction, the political climate in Dover underwent a significant transformation. The African American voter gave the Republican Party, which was at the time the party of Lincoln and emancipation, a significant amount of support. At the same time, the Democratic Party, which was deeply rooted in its southern sympathies, sought to recreate something resembling the pre-war order. During this time, Dover's political scene was particularly dynamic due to the shifting fortunes of various parties and their contacts with the local populace.

The Reconstruction era in Dover is essentially a microcosm of the greater American drama of the time. It captures the conflicting inclinations toward inclusion and exclusivity, the tensions between progress and immobility, and the competing demands for economic stability and fairness. Be they African American activists, white political figures, or regular citizens, Dover residents' decisions during this time period reflected a community navigating the pangs of transformation. Every choice, regardless of whether it was driven by practicality, idealism, or prejudice, helped to create a new social compact that would continue to change through time.

When we look at how Reconstruction affected Dover, we see a city in transition that reflects a country that is itself in transition. Racial equality, economic change, and political realignment were three topics that sprang to the fore at this time and would have an ongoing impact on Dover for years to come. We learn more about Dover's history and the hardships and victories that have shaped its passage through the maze of American history by looking into this crucial time period.

Chapter 11: Dover in the Gilded Age

Dover was in the middle of a period of change, development, and, as the age's name implies, contradictions as the Gilded Age replaced the Reconstruction era. America's industrial prowess reached astounding heights during this period, roughly from the 1870s to the early 1900s, but the shining affluence covered up underlying problems with social inequality and governmental corruption. Dover, too, displayed these societal tendencies in its own particular way, serving as an intriguing microcosm of the country's greater contemporary problems.

The Gilded Age was about creating new patterns that were both beautiful and complicated and weaving them into the fabric of a society that had been torn apart by civil war. Dover changed from being predominantly an agrarian civilization to one with a more varied economy as industrialization and entrepreneurship took hold. Emerging industries complimented agriculture, which remained a pillar. As a result of Dover's advantageous location along the Delaware Railroad, which had developed into a genuine lifeline for the town's commercial goals, factories started to materialize.

Particularly in the peach industry, there was a boom, and for a while, Dover and the state of Delaware dominated the national peach market. The "peach yellows" illness, which devastated the sector, made this success rather temporary. Despite the damage to the peach business, this setback encouraged Dover's farmers to diversify, sowing the seeds for a more hardy agricultural sector that includes apples, berries, and grains.

On the industrial front, an influx of laborers, especially immigrants from Europe, was sparked by the prospect of jobs and financial stability. Small-scale industries including textile mills, machine-specific workshops, and others started to flourish. These developing sectors had a big impact on Dover's economy and social structure, even though they couldn't match the intensity of industrialization witnessed in cities like New York or Chicago.

But not everything that gleamed in Dover during the Gilded Age was gold, much like the larger American environment. The community experienced some social and economic inequality. Men, women, and occasionally even children worked long hours in less-than-ideal conditions as a result of the booming industries' frequent labor exploitation. Grandiose mansions stood close to modest worker cottages as wealth started to concentrate in the hands of a select few, establishing a class stratification that was visible in the town's architecture.

African Americans in Dover faced challenges during this time. Real equality remained elusive despite the legal advancements made during Reconstruction and the abolition of slavery being key turning points. Social segregation was a daily occurrence, and there were still few economic and educational options available. African American churches and schools, on the other hand, began to emerge at this time as hubs of political activism and community life, setting the groundwork for the civil rights battles that would become more intense in the 20th century.

Political favoritism and corruption were widespread throughout the Gilded Age in Dover, but it also laid the seeds for reform. The two main parties competing for control of municipal offices and agendas were the Democratic and Republican parties. Even though politics frequently appeared to be a game for the elites, the problems at hand had a significant impact on Dover citizens' day-to-day lives, whether it was legislation impacting nearby companies, the standard of public education, or the construction of infrastructure like roads and public utilities.

What jumps out about this period of Dover's past is how intricate it was. It was a time that defied simple categorization—one marked by both astounding advancement and glaring inequality. The Gilded Age in Dover was a formative time that defined the town's layout for succeeding generations, whether it was in the humming factories, lush orchards, humble schoolhouses, or the council chambers. appreciation the dynamics of this time period—its successes, failures, ideals, and compromises—gives us not only historical knowledge but also a nuanced appreciation of the complexity that contribute to Dover's status as a distinctive and complicated community today.

Chapter 12: The Rise of Technology and its Effects

The first decades of the 20th century marked an era of technological innovation that forever changed the fabric of American life, and Dover, Delaware was no exception to this transformative wave. The confluence of technology and society is always complex, and in Dover, the effects of technological advances manifested across multiple dimensions: economic structures were overhauled, social dynamics were altered, and the very layout of the city began to change in response to innovations in transport and infrastructure.

In terms of economic change, technology acted as a catalyst that facilitated a shift from traditional agricultural practices to more industrialized methods. The introduction of tractors, mechanical harvesters, and chemical fertilizers revolutionized farming, increasing efficiency but also reducing the need for a large labor force. Consequently, there was a significant movement of people from rural areas to the town, seeking opportunities in Dover's burgeoning factories and businesses.

These factories, too, were sites of technological innovation. The rise of assembly lines, inspired by the likes of Henry Ford, altered the nature of work, with tasks becoming more specialized and efficiency prioritized. These developments, in turn, led to increased production capabilities. Small workshops metamorphosed into larger factories, and new sectors began to take root in Dover. The spread of electricity enabled this transition, lighting up factories for longer hours and powering machinery that made labor less grueling but also less personalized.

While technology created new jobs and increased productivity, it also raised questions about job security, workers' rights, and community integrity. As machines took over tasks that had once required human skill and judgment, labor unions started to gain prominence, advocating for better working conditions and wages that could compete with the allure of mechanical efficiency.

Socially, the rise of technology brought Dover into the modern age in a palpable way. The introduction of the telephone, and later the radio, made the world feel a little smaller, connecting Doverites not just to each other but also to a broader global community. These technologies played an integral role in shaping public opinion, as news could now be disseminated more quickly and broadly than ever before. During times of war or national crisis, this had the effect of unifying the community around common causes or concerns.

Automobiles, perhaps more than any other technology, changed the physical landscape of Dover. The very topology of the city started to adapt to accommodate these new machines. Roads were paved and widened, traffic laws were instituted, and soon enough, the town saw the advent of gas stations, repair shops, and automobile dealerships. The automobile turned previously remote areas into accessible suburbs, forever changing the concept of distance and community in Dover.

Yet, the car culture came with its own set of challenges. While it did democratize mobility, it also contributed to urban sprawl and increased pollution. Moreover, the convenience of personal vehicles began to undermine public transportation systems, a trend that would have long-term implications for social equity and environmental sustainability.

Politically, the rise of technology began to alter the dynamics of governance. Advances in record-keeping and data analysis made governmental processes more efficient but also sparked debates about privacy and surveillance. The rise of the mass media transformed political campaigns, making image and public perception as crucial as policy positions. Government projects to improve or expand infrastructure, often involving new technology, became major points of political debate and public interest.

As we look back on this era, what becomes evident is that technology was not simply a tool for progress; it was a transformative force that reshaped every facet of life in Dover. The town's story during this period serves as a microcosm of broader American trends, illustrating both the promise and the pitfalls of technological advancement. By examining Dover's journey through this era of change, we gain nuanced insights into the complex ways technology intersects with economic, social, and political realms, ultimately shaping the trajectory of communities and nations.

Chapter 13: Dover during WWI and WWII

Dover, Delaware may not be the first place that comes to mind when talking about the two World Wars, but due to its location and infrastructure, it has historically contributed more to American military history than just a footnote. Dover has its own story, one that is intertwined with its population, military airport, and social fabric—belying its ostensibly unremarkable veneer. It wasn't London or Paris, towns under direct siege.

Backtrack to the first decades of the 20th century. Dover, albeit still a minor city, was of strategic importance. The impacts of the impending conflict were already being felt in the city as World War I broke out. America has not yet joined the fighting, despite Europe being engulfed in it. But Dover wasn't left unharmed. People who found work in the expanding manufacturing sector aimed toward war operations abroad started to move into the city. American hammers and lathes were sculpting the machinery before American feet ever set foot on the war-torn lands of Europe.

Then 1917 arrived, and the United States joined World War I. Dover was unexpectedly hit by a spike in enlistments. Many of the young soldiers were from Delaware and were preparing for battle by rehearsing marches and maneuvers. Additionally, the city acted as a small-scale logistics center, gathering supplies including food, textiles, and metals before delivering them to larger depots.

The effect on the soul was profound. Families with strong ties to Dover had to bid their sons goodbye because many of them wouldn't be coming back. The local newspapers were overflowing with pieces that alternated between pro-war propaganda and obituaries for local youngsters. Churches, which were once hubs of fellowship and tranquility, now serve as locations for serious prayers for safe departures.

Dover was first exposed to the hardships and sacrifices of war during World War I, but it was completely turned into a military city during World War II. Dover Army Airfield's construction in 1941 signaled a paradigm shift. The new airfield, which would eventually become Dover Air Force Base, saw much of its use during World War II as a training ground for the crew and pilots of C-47 freight planes. These aircraft were crucial in deploying paratroopers behind enemy lines and supplying troops on the front.

The social structure of the city underwent significant alterations during WWII. The airfield changed the city's demographics and gave it a cosmopolitan feel by drawing servicemen from all over the country. Women have also been placed in positions that were formerly reserved for men. Women took on roles and duties that were too enormous for them when men left to fight, but they did so with a fortitude that would later serve as an inspiration for the feminist movements of the 1960s.

During this time, racial conflict was also present in Dover. When African American personnel were stationed at the airfield, segregation and racial prejudice were terrible realities that the community had to deal with. Civil rights talks were sparked by the war, something Dover and many other American communities had previously ignored.

By the time World War II came to an end, Dover had undergone permanent change. The city's long-term relationship with the military was ensured by the airfield's emergence as a more enduring presence. The city's viewpoints had been enlarged by the conflicts, which made it confront difficult societal issues including gender roles and civil rights.

Although those terrible times were decades ago, Dover's contribution to the World Wars has left an enduring impact. The city may not have been the scene of conflicts or peace agreements, but during those years it acted as a microcosm of American society, feeling the effects of global events in its own unique way.

Therefore, let's not forget about places like Dover—small in size but enormous in their contributions, sacrifices, and lessons—when we think of World War I and World War II. Every ancient portrait, building, and street in this city whispers tales of a history that, in some tiny but crucial ways, influenced not only Dover's future but also the future of the entire globe.

Chapter 14: Military Bases and Economics During WWII

Many American communities were still dealing with the effects of the Great Depression in the years before World War II. The country was plagued by high unemployment, slow economic growth, and an atmosphere of instability. But after that, the war broke out, bringing with it a spike in military spending that turned out to be an unlikely driver of the revival of the economy. Cities all around the nation saw tremendous economic metamorphosis as America's engagement in the war grew, partly as a result of the construction of military bases. One of those cities was Dover, Delaware, the location of the Dover Army Airfield, which served as the forerunner to the Dover Air Force Base.

It was obvious how the airfield's construction had a negative impact on the economy. Jobs in construction appeared fairly immediately. Dover was inundated with a fresh influx of migrant workers as laborers, carpenters, and engineers rushed to the city. Grocery stores, hardware stores, and restaurants in the area prospered as a result of the influx of workers. Due to the surge in housing demand, property values increased dramatically, bringing fresh wealth to the neighborhood. In stark contrast to the depressing economic doldrums that had defined the first half of the decade, the city was bustling with activity.

However, the economic shift went further than only strengthening nearby firms and providing jobs. The construction of the airfield resulted in a long-lasting change in the city's industrial emphasis. Dover was mostly a minor commercial centre that depended on localized trade and agriculture before the war. The city's economy became inextricably linked to military spending with the construction of the airfield. To make radio equipment, airplane parts, and other war-related hardware, small industries sprouted up. These were long-lasting developments that would have an impact on Dover's economy for some time.

The airfield played a crucial role in pilot training and military logistics as the war raged overseas. At all hours, C-47 Skytrain freight planes took off and landed with soldiers, supplies, and occasionally, grimly, casualties. A large support team, including mechanics, radio operators, and medical professionals, was required because to the frequent movement, and many of them were stationed in Dover for the long term. These people made Dover their permanent home; it was no longer merely a place to stay temporarily. New people also brought new requirements, such as for infrastructure, public services, and schools. The city reacted as a result, investing the economic bonanza in construction initiatives that would benefit both the local population and the military personnel.

The city and the airfield coexisted in perfect harmony. Dover provided the military with a strategic location and a ready labor force, and the military gave Dover economic security and the opportunity to diversify its industrial base. But things weren't always easy. Additionally, the town faced challenging moral and social issues as a result of the military's presence. How, for example, does the newly discovered prosperity fit with the ethical consequences of war? Additionally, as we briefly discussed in the last chapter, racial segregation and gender norms came to light, frequently igniting conflict within the community.

The economic environment had fundamentally transformed by the time World War II was over. Cities like Dover had seen a fundamental transformation as a result of the war, which had helped the United States escape the Great Depression. Many people in the post-war years worried that the reduction in military spending would result in economic deterioration, but these worries turned out to be mostly unwarranted. The airfield, which later became the Dover Air Force Base, maintained its economic viability by adjusting to the shifting requirements of the military and, consequently, of the country. The base kept thousands of people employed, and its activities benefited the local economy, ensuring Dover's status as a military city for many years to come.

When we look back, the tale of Dover during World conflict II is a tale of the complex dance between commerce and conflict. It illustrates how military spending serves two purposes: it stimulates economic growth while also posing moral and social dilemmas. And in that story, we discover the tale of America itself: a country propelled by the force of war, permanently changed by its repercussions, yet constantly adjusting and developing. Dover acts as a glass through which we can look at these more general realities, illuminating a complex picture of a city and a nation at a crucial juncture in history.

Chapter 15: Dover in the Civil Rights Era

Dover, like the rest of America, underwent a transformation in the decades that followed World War II. The war's end did not signal a return to the status quo because the city had already seen tremendous economic and social transformation during that time. However, the post-war period brought with it a fresh set of difficulties and opportunities, none more prominent than the nascent Civil Rights Movement. Even though Dover was a long way from the movement's hubs, such as Birmingham, Alabama, or Little Rock, Arkansas, its reverberations were felt strongly in this modest Delaware city.

Dover has long been known as a story of two cities, divided not only by economic class but also by a racial division that dates back to the city's inception. Even though the city was in the north, Jim Crow traditions were still there. Schools and other public spaces were segregated. In a city where the Black community made up a sizeable section of the population, the Dover Army Airfield, later to become the Dover Air Force Base, had likewise been a predominately white institution. However, the military's presence also attracted a variety of people to the city, unintentionally preparing the ground for the discussions and arguments about race that would follow.

African Americans in Dover started to demand fairer legal treatment with the rise of the Civil Rights Movement. Local activists took cues from the larger movement and planned sit-ins and protests that were reminiscent of those occurring in the South. Churches, which had long served as the backbone of the Black community, developed a reputation for being active political hubs. Demands for justice, equality, and the end of segregation were incorporated throughout sermons.

A nonviolent demonstration in front of the State Capitol in Dover in 1961 was one of the noteworthy incidents in the city's Civil Rights history. Students from the area joined activists in calling for an end to school segregation and fair hiring practices during a demonstration. Despite not receiving as much media coverage as some of the larger southern protests, this one was crucial in influencing public sentiment in Delaware. The incident drew the attention of state legislators and prepared the path for upcoming legislative changes intended to improve civil liberties and desegregation.

But not everyone embraced these modifications. People in Dover who opposed the campaign viewed the demands for equality as an insult to the current social structure. The division occasionally took the form of awkward confrontations and even violent acts committed against activists. Even though the city never saw the type of harsh persecution that existed in some Southern states, emotions were high, especially as the movement gained popularity across the country.

The Civil Rights Act of 1964 and the Voting Rights Act of 1965, in particular, were two pieces of federal legislation that the Civil Rights Movement had successfully changed by the late 1960s. These modifications had an immediate effect on Dover. Even though desegregation was a protracted and difficult process, segregation in public schools was eventually prohibited. A more inclusive—though still tense—commercial atmosphere resulted from the prohibition on businesses discriminating against clients based on race.

The Civil Rights Movement in many ways symbolized Dover's coming of age. The city, like the nation, had to face its complicated racial past and take action to create a more fair future. Growing pains were experienced throughout that time, which were interspersed with arguments as well as periods of harmony and understanding.

The Civil Rights Movement's legacy in Dover is still being researched and thought about today. Local and national campaigners have had schools renamed in their honor, and community celebrations frequently mark significant moments in the movement. The fight for equality is still far from over, though. Racial inequality problems still persist, which serves as a reminder of how far we still have to go.

Through the lens of the Civil Rights Movement, we can understand Dover's development as a city that has been shaped and reshaped by historical forces. It serves as a microcosm of America's continuous struggle for racial equality, social justice, and civil liberties—a struggle that, despite being far from over, has irrevocably changed the character of both a city and a country.

Chapter 16: Other Notable Social Movements in Dover

Dover has been formed by a variegated tapestry of social currents that have each contributed to its complicated identity. The Civil Rights Movement was not the only social movement to leave its mark on the city. Dover has served as a stage for societal advancement, even though it frequently follows rather than sets the pace for larger national trends. This is true of the labor movements of the early 20th century, the feminist movements that gained traction in the 1960s and 1970s, up until the environmental and LGBTQ+ rights activism of more recent decades.

The Dover industrial workers and craftsmen became a home for the labor movement in the years after World War I. A significant workforce had been drawn to the growth of manufacturing facilities connected to the war effort, and labor conditions became to be a major source of worry. Dover did see localized protests and strikes, though not on the same magnitude as other American cities. Workers' activism helped lay the foundation for the employment norms we take for granted today by advocating for greater pay, more equitable hours, and safer working conditions.

Dover was influenced by the feminist movement in the 1960s and 1970s, albeit in more subdued ways. Dover was a place where traditional gender norms had been prescribed and accepted for a very long time, much like the rest of the country. However, many of the women who had entered the labor during World War II were hesitant to give up their economic freedom. Groups and community forums began formed in the city to talk about topics including equal pay, reproductive rights, and job discrimination as a result of the national women's liberation movement. The women of Dover were a part of the rising tide that swept the country, despite the fact that the city may not have been the focus of feminist movement.

Environmental issues have sparked activity in Dover in more recent decades. As a coastal state, Delaware faces particular problems brought on by climate change, such as increasing sea levels and a rise in the frequency of severe weather occurrences. Local activism has frequently emphasized conservation and sustainable development, with a number of projects aiming to protect Delaware's natural surroundings. As a result of increased public awareness of environmental issues, community clean-ups, tree-planting celebrations, and educational forums on sustainability have become commonplace.

Additionally, Dover has seen an increase in LGBTQ+ activity, particularly in the twenty-first century. The fight for job equality, marital equality, and societal acceptance has active supporters throughout the city. The inclusion of Pride celebrations on Dover's cultural calendar signifies a broader societal movement in favor of inclusivity. It's crucial to remember that these developments weren't without difficulties. Progress in LGBTQ+ rights has encountered resistance from conservative groups, as with other social movements, making the accomplishments all the more noteworthy.

Notably, waves of immigration have also had an impact on Dover's social fabric. Dover has experienced a constant influx of immigrants from various cultures, each of whom has added to the city's variety even if it is not a big immigration hub in comparison to other American cities. This has resulted in a modest but significant immigrant rights activist movement, which is evident in the community outreach initiatives, cultural celebrations, and naturalization ceremonies that have come to characterize contemporary Dover.

So even though Dover might not come to mind when considering social activity, the city has a past filled with important movements that have shaped its complex identity. Every wave of movement has left its imprint, moving the city closer to a future that is both equal and inclusive.

Dover in many respects serves as a microcosm of the multiplicity of socioeconomic forces that have shaped America. It serves as evidence of the effectiveness of group efforts and the manner in which regular individuals may have a significant impact on remarkable transformations. Its tale serves as a reminder that societal development frequently results from innumerable minor fights, each of which shaped history in a different way. It is a story about both the smaller revolutions that take place when a society decides it is time for change as well as the major events that grab headlines.

Chapter 17: Technological Revolution of the 20th Century to the Millennium

Dover, like the rest of the United States, found itself caught up in a technological revolution that fundamentally changed every area of life as the 20th century came to an end and the new millennium got underway. This chapter offers a fascinating overview of how technology—particularly the development of the personal computer and the internet—has changed the social dynamics, economic climate, and very pulse of daily life in Dover. It is the tale of how a city swept up in the currents of technological change discovered fresh ways to develop, communicate, and express oneself.

The personal computer era began in the late 1970s and early 1980s. Personal computers started to enter the homes of common people as they became more accessible and affordable. This had a significant impact on the job market in Dover. The emergence of data entry employment, computer repair businesses, and software development businesses. Local schools began include computer education in their curricula, fully aware that having a working knowledge of this new technology was not only advantageous but also essential for the younger generation.

But the real turning point for Dover came with the development of the internet in the 1990s. The internet, which was once only used by government and academic institutions, has evolved into a platform for commerce and social interaction with virtually endless potential. Dover's enterprises were suddenly able to access a global market. Mom-and-pop shops create websites to advertise their goods to clients outside of the city borders. Even the Dover Air Force Base, a facility so essential to the city's character, used the internet to modernize its processes and increase the effectiveness of everything from personnel administration to logistics.

The social effects of the internet were equally significant. For starters, it altered how residents of Dover interacted with one another and the outside world. Social media sites and online discussion forums have developed into spaces for advocacy, community building, and discussion. For Dover's different social groups, from environmental causes to LGBTQ+ rights, this democratization of communication had particular relevance because it gave them a bigger stage and a wider audience than ever before.

The technological revolution did, however, not come without its difficulties and setbacks. Local stores were in danger of losing customers as e-commerce grew. The distance between those who have access to the internet and those who do not has grown more pronounced, known as the "digital divide." Low-income families and the elderly, who were already at a disadvantage in a world that was rapidly growing digital, were particularly concerned about this.

The surge of technical development continued as the twenty-first century got underway. Smartphones, super-fast internet, and a wide range of digital services had all become commonplace in Dover. In reaction to these technical developments, local governance also started to shift. Online portals for obtaining public services, such as renewing vehicle registrations or making utility payments, have become commonplace, providing citizens with a new level of efficiency and convenience.

Additionally, the development of technology opened up unanticipated paths for economic diversification. For instance, due to the city's cheaper cost of living in comparison to other conventional tech centres like Silicon Valley, Dover has become home to a number of small digital businesses. With its focus on technology development, the Air Force Base's presence acted as a magnet for luring tech-based businesses.

The city's cultural and leisure sectors were likewise touched by the technological revolution. Dover's libraries have evolved from being only book storage facilities to multifunctional community hubs that provide free internet access, digital workshops, and a variety of online resources. Free Wi-Fi was installed in parks and public areas, increasing their attractiveness to younger, tech-savvy generations.

The tale of Dover in the digital age is, in many respects, a microcosm of America's more general experience with the digital revolution. It captures all of the thrills, chances, difficulties, and even perils that come with living in a world that is experiencing rapid technological change. It gives a clear impression of a metropolis that is always changing and reinventing itself to match the parameters of a new digital environment.

Beyond simply bringing Dover into the modern era, the technological revolution rewired the very DNA of the city, changing how its residents interact with one another, work, and interact with the outside world. It's a shift that keeps happening, with each new innovation bringing with it a new set of opportunities and difficulties. Dover continues to be an ardent player in this developing story, constantly gazing to the horizon.

Chapter 18: Changing Demographics and Culture of the 20th Century to the Millennium

Residents of the city today would find the Dover that existed at the turn of the 20th century to be essentially unrecognizable. This is caused by a significant shift in the city's demographics and culture as well as changes in the political climate and technological breakthroughs. Dover changed over a century, echoing changes that took place across the country, from a tiny, rather homogenous town to a cosmopolitan, varied city.

Dover's early 20th-century population was largely of European heritage and was very homogeneous. Agriculture, small-scale industries, and a growing military presence dominated the economy. Community institutions including churches, Rotary Clubs, and regional affiliates of national organizations dominated social life. The majority of the population was Protestant, and Anglo-Saxon influences could be found frequently at community gatherings.

However, Dover witnessed an infusion of military people from many backgrounds as the United States got more involved in international conflicts, beginning with World War I and peaking with World War II. Dover Air Force Base's establishment and expansion had an impact on the city's economy as well as its diverse population. Armed forces personnel from all around the United States and subsequently the world settled in Dover, frequently bringing their families with them.

The Great Migration was yet another huge demographic upheaval that occurred after World War II. African Americans who were escaping the oppressive conditions and ingrained prejudice of the Southern states began to settle in Dover, like many other Northern communities. The steady growth of the Black population added a fresh dimension to Dover's cultural mosaic. The number and influence of churches that had previously catered primarily to Black parishioners increased, enhancing the city's religious and social scene.

In the latter decades of the 20th century, a wider variety of newcomers—including those from Latin America, Asia, and Africa—started to populate the area. Public schools in Dover started to reflect this diversity. Schools had to accommodate kids whose primary language was Spanish, Tagalog, or Swahili even while English remained the predominant language. Along with typical American cuisine, the city's culinary offerings increased to include anything from Vietnamese pho to Mexican tacos.

The arts and entertainment sector was likewise impacted by the shift in demographics. Multicultural festivals, ethnic food fairs, and a range of musical and theatrical acts that highlighted many cultures were added to what had previously been a simple lineup of fairs, church bazaars, and military parades.

Dover was struggling with the intricacies of its new identity around the turn of the millennium. Diversity was celebrated more and more, but it also presented problems. The city had to figure out how to deal with the challenges of having a diversified society while also integrating different communities. This included dealing with racial conflicts and social inequities that grew increasingly obvious as the city's population varied, as well as instituting English as a Second Language (ESL) programs in schools.

Additionally, the idea of community itself evolved. The church, the school, or the neighborhood club were frequently the centers of social life in past decades. But with the advent of the internet and increased mobility in the late 20th century, social networks had both grown and become more dispersed. People felt community not simply because they lived close to one another but also because of shared views, ethnic backgrounds, and hobbies.

Dover's identity was changing as the new millennium rolled around. The city expanded beyond the sum of its historical sites, military installation, and agricultural heritage. It evolved into a kaleidoscope of many cultures, customs, and histories, each of which added a distinctive hue to the overall picture.

What does all of this mean for Dover, then? It denotes a more complex, multi-layered identity that is continually revised and reinvented. It refers to a location that is more in tune with the globalized, linked world of the twenty-first century. But more crucially, it denotes a city that has mastered—and is continuously mastering—the art of adapting to change and growth, welcoming the difficulties that come its way.

One thing is certain as we stand on the threshold of this new era: the Dover of the future will be molded not simply by its institutions or topography, but also by the diverse population that calls it home. They are the key players in this dynamic novel, and the sum of their individual tales tells the tale of Dover.

Chapter 19: Post-9/11 Dover

The horrific events of September 11, 2001, rippled across the country and profoundly changed the fabric of the country. This was also true of Dover. Residents of this city, which has a sizable military presence, felt the effects instantly and strongly. The years following 9/11 were a turning point in Dover's history, with increased security at the Dover Air Force Base and a rise in local patriotism and community support.

After the bombings, Dover Air Force Base, which had long served as the city's identity's center, took on an even more crucial role. It served as the initial location for receiving the remains of service members who died in the ensuing conflicts in Afghanistan and Iraq because it was one of the principal ports for the U.S. military's mortuary services. As convoys routinely traveled to the base, this served as a sobering and persistent reminder of the human cost of war for the citizens of Dover. In order to honor the dead and their families, the neighborhood frequently joined together for memorial services and to line the streets with American flags.

There were various changes made to the base itself. What had previously been a rather open post was transformed into a guarded compound, and military families saw a noticeable increase in security checks for both on-base living and daily activities. The increasing operating pace also meant that service members stationed at Dover had longer and more frequent deployments, which had an effect on neighborhood families and the larger community. The base's duties increased as well, with a focus on providing logistical support for Middle Eastern operations.

In the years following 9/11, changes in the local community outside of the military context were subtle but significant. Dover's local government organizations and first responders took part in federal initiatives created to prepare for potential terrorist attacks, natural disasters, or other calamities during a time of increasing national vigilance and fear. Community policing was given more attention, and readiness education programs were becoming frequent.

Like the rest of the nation, the city experienced a rise in patriotism. Flags were flown from buildings, commercial spaces, and vehicles. To foster a sense of pride in one's country and an awareness of democratic values, the local schools increased the amount of American history and civics taught in their curricula. Veterans Day, Memorial Day, and the Fourth of July were more heavily observed, enthusiastically honored, and attended by more Dover residents than in previous years.

The surge in patriotism also brought its own share of complications, particularly in a multicultural and developing city like Dover. Residents' attitudes toward one another changed subtly but noticeably as a result of the climate of increased national security, particularly against persons from backgrounds or religions that some sections of the society deemed "foreign." Muslims and anyone with Middle Eastern ancestry frequently came under more scrutiny. Racial profiling and discriminatory incidents did happen, showing the shadowy underbelly of a society on high alert.

The role of educational institutions was vital in negotiating this perilous terrain. Schools in Dover were used as forums to talk about the difficulties of terrorism, extremism, and national identity. Education has become a transforming instrument in influencing the perspectives of the next generation on diversity and inclusion as dialogue about the value of tolerance and understanding has been incorporated into school settings.

Dover experienced the knock-on effects of a nation at war and on high alert economically. Defense and homeland security-related federal contracts proliferated, giving the local economy a cash boost but also tying it more tightly to the ups and downs of federal expenditure and military deployments. Military families moving in and out of the area had an impact on everything from retail to real estate, producing a demographic that is economically significant but relatively ephemeral.

Dover entered a moment of contemplation following 9/11, reevaluating what it meant to be a town in a country going through quick, frightening change. The expansion of the military, a heightened sense of patriotism accompanied by internal strife, and the shifting economic conditions brought on by a nation at war all contributed to a city's struggle to establish itself in a novel and unsettling environment.

But despite all of its difficulties and complexity, this time period also demonstrated the tenacity and adaptability that have always been defining characteristics of Dover's history. Dover continued to engage with the challenging issues, maintaining an active participant in the molding of its own destiny and that of the country it calls home, whether through communal gatherings to remember dead soldiers or discussions about the fundamental foundation of American principles in school classrooms.

Chapter 20: Contemporary Challenges and Opportunities

Dover is faced with a variety of chances and challenges as it navigates the intricacies of the 21st century, which may very well define its future course. Dover, like many American communities, struggles with concerns of economic injustice, global warming, social fairness, and the on-going effects of rapid technological development. However, these difficulties also present special chances for development, invention, and community building.

Start by talking about the economics. Dover was severely impacted by the financial crisis of 2008, which resulted in employment losses, home foreclosures, and a reduction in public services. The incident left a lasting impression on the city's communal psyche even if the economy has substantially recovered. Economic stability is still a concern, particularly as conventional industries decline and businesses powered by technology grow. Dover has the chance to make the most of its distinctive qualities—such as its location near a military installation and its standing as the state capital of Delaware—in order to draw funding to industries like technology, renewable energy, and healthcare. Economic difficulties can be transformed into sources of prosperity by making investments in workforce development, promoting collaborations between academic institutions and enterprises, and fostering an atmosphere that is friendly to small firms.

An other pressing concern is climate change. Even though Dover is not located on the shore, it is nonetheless susceptible to the effects of sea level rise because Delaware is one of the states most at risk in the United States. Infrastructure resilience needs to be heavily invested in due to an increase in the frequency of extreme weather events like hurricanes and flooding. Herein lies a chance for Dover to set the bar high for sustainability. The city could serve as a model for how cities can proactively handle environmental concerns by adopting renewable energy sources and encouraging eco-friendly practices among its citizens and companies.

The topic of social justice is another. Dover's diverse population contributes to its energy and rich cultural diversity, but it also means that racial and economic inequality are challenges that cannot be overlooked. Dover has the ability to be at the vanguard of change as the nation as a whole struggles with demands for social fairness and reform. Systemic problems can be addressed in a significant way via community interaction, police reform, and educational programs targeted at decreasing the achievement gap. The city has access to an enormous wealth of different ideas and potential answers thanks to the very diversity that presents issues.

Finally, we reach technology, which is a double-edged tool like no other. On the one hand, the digital age presents unheard-of prospects for business innovation, streamlined government operations, and interconnectedness on a global scale. The digital gap, the possibility of job loss owing to automation, and data privacy concerns, on the other hand, are significant concerns. The issue for Dover is to adopt technology in a way that improves rather than degrades the standard of living for its citizens.

In Dover, public and private organizations can work together to develop tech-based solutions for better healthcare, transportation, and civic involvement while also funding initiatives that will help the workforce become more tech-savvy. Dover Air Force Base's presence in the area, with its focus on cutting-edge technology, might serve as a catalyst for creativity, drawing tech firms and highly qualified individuals to the area.

It's important to keep in mind that cities are living things that constantly change in response to the opportunities and difficulties they face as we think about the future. This is also true of Dover. The city's past serves as evidence of its resiliency, adaptability, and steadfast sense of community. Yes, there are many challenges, but there are also many chances for those who are ready to take them. The potential of what Dover can become—a city that celebrates its illustrious past while audaciously forging ahead—lies in the delicate balance between the two.

The decisions taken today by decision-makers, community leaders, and regular residents will have an impact on Dover for years to come. This time gives a rare opportunity to rethink what this city stands for, how it functions, and what it is capable of accomplishing. It is a time that is both full of tremendous problems and thrilling potential. It's a story that is still being written, one that is rife with possibility while yet being full of uncertainty. And that's possibly the most thrilling tale of them all.

Chapter 21: Famous Personalities from Dover

It's impossible to overlook the people who have come from this diverse city to leave a lasting impression on the rest of the world as you delve into Dover's history and culture. These individuals exhibit an intriguing variety of skills, from politics and military service to the arts and sports, each adding to the depth of Dover's legacy.

Judge William Henry Harrison Ross will be our first case. Ross, a Delaware governor from 1851 to 1855, was born in 1827. Despite being a supporter of slavery at the time and belonging to the Democratic Party, his government was renowned for its economic discipline and for having spearheaded reforms in public education. Ross remains a key character in Delaware's political history, highlighting the intricacies of Dover's past, particularly when it comes to racial and political concerns, despite the fact that his later years were hampered by financial difficulties and his loyalty to the Confederacy.

Delino DeShields, a native of Delaware, is well-known in the world of athletics. Despite being from Seaford, DeShields has deep ties to the city of Dover thanks to his prodigious charity efforts there. DeShields, a former Major League Baseball player, spent his career with organizations including the Los Angeles Dodgers and the Montreal Expos. His efforts to encourage child sports and education in Dover and its neighboring villages have had an influence off the field.

General Henry H. Arnold has a distinguished career in the military. Arnold, a Pennsylvania native, served at Dover Air Force Base where he was instrumental in making it one of the biggest air command posts in the country. As the Commander of the U.S. Army Air Forces, he went on to become one of the few five-star generals in American history and played a crucial role in World War II. He has had a significant impact on Dover, the nation as a whole, and the air base where he works.

Notable figures in the arts are also connected to Dover. Robert Crumb, a well-known cartoonist and musician recognized for his subversive and satirical aesthetic, is one such person. While Crumb was raised in Dover and attended high school there, he was actually born in Philadelphia. Even though he eventually moved away, the years he spent growing up in Dover had a profound effect on his writing, providing yet another prism through which to comprehend the city's complex cultural influence.

It's also important to highlight Annie Jump Cannon, an astronomer who was born in Dover in 1863. She transformed the way we categorize stars now while working at the Harvard College Observatory. Cannon, who was partially deaf, surmounted the restrictions placed on women by her era to achieve important advancements in the astronomy field. She was a trailblazer in both science and breaking down gender barriers, serving as an inspiration for future generations of scientists, particularly female students.

The 46th President of the United States, former Vice President Joe Biden, is last but by no means least. Though he was raised in Delaware, where he later served as the state's U.S. Senator for 36 years, Biden was really born in Scranton, Pennsylvania. Though Biden is more frequently linked to Wilmington, the capital and largest city of Delaware, Dover has absorbed the full force of his political influence. By extension, Dover received renewed interest as a result of Biden's election to the president, which put the city in the national and even international focus.

These people are just a small sample of the famous people with connections to or significant influence in Dover. Each one offers a tale about their environment as well as their individual accomplishments. To Dover's own story, their lives and professions in turn add depths of complexity and richness, creating a picture of a place that has nurtured talent, ambition, and influence in a variety of fields.

Chapter 22: Dover as Seen on TV

When discussing Dover as a media entity, we frequently need to look a little further, eschewing the flash and glamour of locations that are frequently considered to be "more telegenic." But for those who take the time to look, Dover has permanently shaped several facets of television and, to a lesser extent, movies. These roles play a significant influence in how this small but significant city integrates into the greater fabric of American life.

Focusing on Dover International Speedway will help. This monster of NASCAR racing is frequently seen in sports coverage, especially during the "Monster Energy NASCAR Cup Series," when it receives its fair share of airtime on FOX and NBC. In addition to these high-profile live events, the track has also been featured in reality TV series about the auto racing industry, such the History Channel's "Counting Cars," where the hosts occasionally talk about races that have taken place at the Speedway. The TV appearances of Dover International Speedway convey the tale of a city that thrives on speed, competition, and the American fascination with automobile culture even though the track has yet to make its big-screen debut.

The important military center, Dover Air Force Base, has been featured in a number of documentaries and news specials. The post makes some of its most moving appearances in PBS's "American Experience" shows that focus on military history, where the facility is frequently mentioned for its contribution to operations and logistics. Events at Dover AFB have also been covered by CNN and Fox News, particularly when solemn transfer ceremonies for deceased servicemen are held. These events, which were shown live on television, give Dover a sense of seriousness and significance that transcends its status as a little city.

Dover has occasionally featured programming that is more lifestyle-focused. Cooking programs like Food Network's "Diners, Drive-Ins and Dives" have highlighted regional restaurants, highlighting the variety of cuisines available in Dover, from seafood specialties to international cuisines, despite their lack of popularity. Dover has been featured in travel programs from networks like the Travel Channel and even YouTube vloggers, with a focus on its historical sites and cultural attractions.

There aren't many fictional depictions of Dover, which is true. The city hasn't served as the central location for a well-liked TV show or motion picture, although it has been mentioned in passing in dramas and criminal procedurals like "NCIS" or "Law & Order," frequently as an unremarkable locale connected to a military case or as a representation of small-town America. Even though these portrayals are brief, they occasionally tell a story. They demonstrate how Dover is frequently used as a metaphor for larger American themes like militarism, small-town ideals, or the monotony of everyday life.

There are several ways to interpret Dover's relative dearth of scripted media. It might be a missed chance for storytellers to explore a city full with untold stories and intricate cultural relations. However, this absence also poses a challenge and an invitation for artists to delve deeper into a city that captures all parts of the American experience, from its military significance to its growing diversity.

In the end, Dover's appearances on television and in movies, albeit brief, constitute a collection of fragmented but illuminating pictures. These fleeting moments reflect the spirit of a city that quietly but significantly adds to the American tale in its own special manner. Dover comes out as a complex character who merits a closer examination, both on and off the screen, whether it's the scream of motors at the Speedway or the solemn rituals at the Air Force Base.

Chapter 23: Dover as Depicted in Literature

Despite not being featured as extensively as some other cities, Dover has had the distinct honor and task of being immortalized in print. However, despite its more infrequent appearances, it does so in works that significantly advance our understanding of this Delaware capital.

"The Travels of William Bartram," a travel journal written by American naturalist William Bartram in the 18th century, is one of the main publications that discusses Dover. This historical book mentions Dover as a stop in Bartram's larger exploration of the American Southeast even though it is not fiction. We can see how Dover and the surroundings were viewed in the early years of the Republic through his observations of the flora, animals, and Lenape people.

Dover is regularly mentioned as a crucial political and economic hub in William H. Williams' book "Slavery and Freedom in Delaware, 1639-1865" in relation to the state's involvement in slavery and eventual freedom. Dover is depicted in the book as a place of both oppression and emancipation, illuminating the town's multifaceted role during one of America's most ethically and socially complicated periods.

While not situated in Dover, the mystery book "Patient Zero" by Jonathan Maberry does have significant sequences at Dover Air Force Base. The military installation is shown as a center of urgent activity, emphasizing its significance for national security. The Dover Air Force Base is a genuine, crucial location that gives the imaginary catastrophe more weight. The book draws on post-9/11 worries.

The anthology "Delaware Poetry Review," which occasionally includes writers who poignantly alludes to Dover, details its vistas and quiet street corners as a backdrop to more in-depth existential inquiries. Dover also appears there in a more lyrical form. The anthology frequently include works by regional poets, evoking a feeling of place that includes Dover and its distinctive characteristics.

Dover serves as the setting for court hearings in Ann Rule's true crime book, "And Never Let Her Go: Thomas Capano: The Deadly Seducer," about a murder case that shook Delaware. Although not the main site of the story, the city serves as the scene where justice is administered, providing yet another layer to Dover's intricate social structure.

Dover may be mentioned in instructional literature for young adults, especially in works that discuss Delaware's significance in early American history. Dover is mentioned as a significant place for American independence and the ratification of the Constitution in books like "Delaware: The First State" by Carol E. Hoffecker, offering historical context that young minds can cling onto.

The variety of genres that Dover occurs in, from historical literature to mystery fiction to actual crime, is remarkable. This illustrates the variety of ways Dover interacts with wider

American narratives: as a historical place, a military installation, a venue for social justice, and the regular setting for shocking and provocative murders.

Although there is a clear sense that Dover's literary tapestry is still unfinished and has potential for new voices and stories that can explore the city's shifting intricacies. The unwritten works of the future offer an exciting possibility for a more thorough and nuanced picture, whether they explore Dover's expanding immigrant communities or analyze its interaction with the altering American environment.

Despite its small size, the city of Dover holds a special position in literature because of its broad scope and significance. It serves as a metaphor, an actor, and a platform for bigger historical, social, and psychological topics to be explored. Dover is more than just a location—as these books and other pieces of literature demonstrate—it is also a complex character in and of itself.

Chapter 24: Iconic Dover Landmarks and History

Dover's famous landmarks serve as the cornerstones of the city's past and future in a location rich in history where cobblestone streets and modernism coexist. Even though it's simple to pass by these landmarks, each one has a tale to tell, and these tales capture the very heart of Dover—a city steeped in its past but always changing.

For instance, the Dover Green serves as a virtual time machine that whisks tourists back to the 18th century. The Green, which is surrounded by vintage structures and a historic courthouse, has seen important occasions including pro-independence demonstrations during the American Revolution and Delaware's ratification of the U.S. Constitution. As a physical representation of the democratic ideas that have influenced Dover and the country at large, it has remained a gathering spot for political events, protests, and local celebrations across time.

The Old State House is a short distance away and exudes respect. The Georgian-style building, which was constructed in 1791, has been used for a variety of governmental activities, including parliamentary and judicial hearings. It has been restored to its former splendor and is now used as a museum. The murmurs of the men and women who made significant contributions to Delaware's statecraft can be heard echoing through its halls. Despite this, it is more than just a museum because it was still in service for legislative purposes in 1933, serving as a link between past and contemporary governance.

Another intriguing site that relates a more contemporary but no less significant story is the Johnson Victrola Museum. With his mechanical inventions, businessman and inventor E.R. Johnson transformed the record business. The museum captures the entrepreneurial spirit that adds to Dover's unique culture, demonstrating how innovation and business savvy have contributed impacted the city's fabric, even though it may not be directly related to important historical events.

Another type of landmark, Dover Air Force Base, stands as a contemporary memorial to the nation's and the city's military obligations. Beyond its obvious strategic significance, the base has strong ties to the neighborhood and offers both economic and cultural support. Dover is made sombre by its presence because it serves as the base for humanitarian missions and the homecoming of fallen servicemen.

The "Monster Mile," also referred to as Dover International Speedway, is more than just a racetrack. It's a hub of culture that combines the excitement of sports with a sense of belonging. Dover becomes a bustling hub of activity on race weekends, and the Speedway takes on the role of the city's beating heart. It displays the city's passion for sports and also represents tenacity and rivalry that seem distinctly American.

Delaware State University stands for the city's dedication to education and social mobility in a more academic context. The school, which was established in 1891 as a land-grant college for African Americans, serves as a reminder of Dover's complicated racial history and its efforts to promote inclusiveness and equality. The university's expansive campus and expanding impact serve as a symbol of opportunity, desire, and the future of the city.

Dover's numerous churches, synagogues, and mosques reveal yet another aspect of its religious and spiritual heritage. These houses of worship may not be as "iconic" in the conventional sense, but they are nevertheless very important to Dover's social structure. They embody the diversity of human experience and belief that converges in this city, from the historically significant Christ Church, which dates back to 1734, to younger religious institutions serving a growingly diverse population.

These landmarks tell the story of Dover's complex character in their own unique ways. They serve as tangible representations of a past that includes colonial conflicts, racial tensions, technological advancements, bravery in the military, sporting triumphs, and spiritual pursuits. When combined, they create a mosaic that offers a complete picture of Dover—a city that is constantly cognizant of its colorful past while actively crafting its future.

Chapter 25: Architecture of Dover

Dover's architecture speaks for itself when it comes to the city's complex history and wide-ranging cultural influences. It offers a literal and metaphorical physical illustration of how the city has changed throughout the ages, according to diverse socio-economic, technological, and aesthetic currents. If you pay attention, the built environment in Dover will tell you stories about a city that has changed yet still has remnants of its past at every turn.

Let's start with the colonial past that is so deeply ingrained in Dover's built environment. Some of the city's most historically noteworthy structures are in the Georgian style, which was popular in the late 18th century. The Old State House, a magnificently preserved building from 1791, is one example of how Georgian architectural principles are demonstrated. Its symmetrical design, brick façade, and classical ornamental elements are all hallmarks of Georgian architecture. It serves as a visual clue that takes viewers back to a time when democracy and statecraft were just being started.

However, Georgian is not the only colonial design that endured. The Colonial Revival style is also evident throughout the city, especially in the gable roofs, classical columns, and restrained adornment of residential homes. These older-style houses, which are frequently seen in Dover's older neighborhoods, provide a sense of continuity by tying the present to a recent history.

Dover's architectural story takes a Gothic turn when we enter the 19th century. Numerous churches in the city, such as Christ Church and Wesley United Methodist Church, feature Gothic Revival design features such pointed arches, elaborate woodwork, and decorative tracery. These structures are more than just houses of worship; via their exalting forms and minute workmanship, they are architectural anthems that sing homage to the sky.

New architectural movements and the winds of industrialization arrived around the turn of the 20th century. In some residential neighborhoods, the Arts & Crafts movement's impact can be evident. These dwellings, with their focus on handiwork, natural materials, and harmonious landscape integration, indicate a backlash against industrial mass production and a yearning for simplicity before the industrial revolution. They are nostalgic yet reassuring—the architectural equivalent of a sigh.

The Modernist influence started to become apparent by the middle of the 20th century. Modernist concepts are embraced by structures with clean lines, practical designs, and plain surfaces like the Dover Public Library and a few of the ones at Delaware State University. These structures, which are frequently composed of steel, glass, and concrete, offer a striking contrast to the earlier historical designs, yet they are nonetheless important. They represent the city's readiness to change and grow, to look to the future while letting go of the past.

But Dover is more than just a patchwork of many historical trends; it also exhibits distinctive regional adaptations. Think about how Dover Air Force Base, a blend of functional design and a hint of institutional solemnity, was influenced by the military style. Similar to the military institution they house, these are not overtly attention-grabbing structures, but rather ones that convey their owners' intentions and purposes.

Sustainable architecture has become more popular recently, reflecting a greater awareness of environmental challenges around the world. Rooftop solar panels are becoming more common, and energy-efficient building designs are being used in recent construction. It is an architectural change that represents both the development of social consciousness and technological progress.

Dover's architectural landscape has changed throughout time, displaying a variety of influences from colonial to modern, from reverent to practical, from sentimental to forward-thinking. It's a city where the past and the present coexist together, each leaving its imprint without overwhelming the other. In this way, Dover's architecture is more than just a collection of structures; it is a living, breathing organism that personifies the city's nuanced character, its successes and setbacks, and its never-ending search for identity in a constantly shifting environment.

Chapter 26: Key Industries of Economic Evolution

The economic foundations of Dover, like those of any flourishing community, have been varied and dynamic, adapting to changes in both regional demands and international markets. In the 18th and early 19th centuries, the economy was predominately agrarian. Since then, it has undergone a number of transformations to take on its current form, which includes an unusual fusion of the public sector, the private sector, and the service sector, among others. The intriguing development of Dover's major sectors reflects not just the growth of the city but also broader economic tendencies that have affected the country as a whole.

Agriculture was the backbone of Dover's economy in its early years. Delaware's lush land was ideal for a variety of farming operations, from grain to livestock. The ability to fish and gather oysters was further facilitated by the area's proximity to rivers. Early Dover was centered on farms and fisheries, and local festivals honoring the abundance of land and water continue to remember its significance.

The development of railroads in the 19th century started to diversify Dover's economic environment. Now that goods could be carried farther and faster, new markets could be reached, and the city could become a logistical hub. The Delaware Railroad Company, founded in 1852, gave the neighborhood's companies the much-needed boost they required, and for a period, Dover experienced a boom in minor manufacturing facilities. A burgeoning population and a varied economy led to the emergence of textile, glass, and carpenter businesses. The railroad connected Dover to the greater intellectual and cultural currents of the country by transporting not only products but also ideas.

With the creation of Dover Air Force Base in 1941, the 20th century saw the beginning of yet another transformation. The base not only played a crucial role in America's security system, but it also had a big impact on the neighborhood's economy. Military personnel and their families arrived in huge numbers, which led to an increase in demand for housing, schools, shops, and other services. Over time, the base grew to be the biggest employer in the community, changing the demographics and reorienting the city's economy toward the military and related sectors.

Healthcare and education became major economic players in the second half of the 20th century and the beginning of the 21st. Along with other educational institutions, Delaware State University has developed into a force in both academia and business, employing both faculty and staff and drawing in visitors who boost the regional economy. Along with the aging of the population and the expansion of medical specialties, healthcare services have increased. The economic environment of Dover currently includes hospitals and healthcare facilities as essential elements.

Due in part to landmarks like the Dover International Speedway, the service sector, in especially the hospitality and tourism sectors, has grown in importance. The weekends of the races see an increase in tourists who fill the hotels, eateries, and shops. The local economy now depends heavily on tourism, which also offers transient but significant job prospects.

Let's not undervalue the importance of startups and small enterprises. These enterprises offer depth and resiliency to Dover's economic character because they are driven by regional inventiveness and frequently serve niche markets. These businesses, which range from artisanal shops to Internet companies, represent the entrepreneurial spirit of America in miniature.

Dover's economy now is as diverse as its past and present. The city's economy is woven together from a variety of old and contemporary enterprises, each adding its own distinct shade. As a result of demographic changes, technology improvements, and shifting consumer preferences, this diversification has both been a response to them and a driving force behind them.

The economic development of Dover makes for an intriguing case study in flexibility, resiliency, and vision. From its agricultural beginnings to its current varied economy, the city has managed to develop while preserving its fundamental principles and sense of community. Dover is a symbol of the opportunities that might arise when a town is open to change while maintaining a strong sense of its identity and traditions.

Chapter 27: Dover in the National and Global Economy

Dover noticed that it was becoming more intertwined with the fabric of a wider national and international economy as the 21st century unfurled its uncertainties and potential. Dover was now a part of a complicated global network of economic, cultural, and technological interactions, and it could no longer be considered merely an outpost of local and regional significance. While this transformation offered opportunities for growth and development, it also exposed the city to a new set of difficulties and factors to take into account.

Since the turn of the century, Dover's financial institutions have evolved from traditional banking models to diversified financial services that range from investment services to mortgage lending. This is in line with larger national trends. But the 2008 global financial crisis was a stark reminder of how linked these economic systems are. Dover's banks and companies were not exempt from the fallout from Wall Street's collapse. There were layoffs, business closures, and a noticeable tension in the air, despite the fact that the city didn't face the same levels of economic misery as some other regions of the country.

In part due to the tenacity of neighborhood companies and government programs intended to spur economic growth, the recovery was gradual but steady. These varied from infrastructure spending aimed at luring larger enterprises to tax incentives for small businesses. Through these initiatives, Dover began to restore its economic footing, albeit in a setting that had been permanently affected by factors on a global scale.

Manufacturing in Dover, which was previously the engine of the regional economy, faced difficult obstacles as more and more jobs were being outsourced to nations with lower labor prices. This wasn't just a local problem; it was a sign of broader economic trends that were hurting towns and cities all around the country. To survive, Dover has to change. While other businesses changed to service-based business models, some corporations redirected their attention to specific manufacturing niches where they could still maintain a competitive edge. Recognizing the growing significance of the digital economy, the city also made an effort to recruit internet companies and startups.

Additionally, international trade agreements and multinational enterprises influenced the economic history of Dover. The dynamic between import and export became essential to the local economy. Dover enjoyed a logistical advantage due to its closeness to important ports and transportation hubs, making it a desirable location for companies engaged in international trade.

The city also discovered itself in a global talent and market competition at the same time. Dover had to make investments in education and worker training because of the development of remote work and the capacity to collaborate across geographies to remain competitive in a global market.

Initiatives for STEM education in public schools and collaborations between regional industries and colleges were all part of this.

Similar to how technological advancements had influenced developments in Dover's past, they are still influencing its economic environment. Advances in artificial intelligence, automation, and e-commerce have produced both opportunities and difficulties. Local businesses found it difficult to compete with online juggernauts, but they also discovered innovative ways to contact clients online. Automation increased productivity, but it also raised worries about job loss.

Dover finds itself at a risky and exciting economic crossroads as the twenty-first century progresses. Future success of the company depends on its capacity to adjust to quickly changing national and international economic environments. Many external forces will continue to have an impact, including financial markets, technological developments, and climate change, among others. But as history has proven, Dover has a strong character and a talent for adapting. The city will be led by this combination of adaptation and resilience as it negotiates its position in the increasingly interconnected global economy.

Chapter 28: Notable Companies in Dover

A few names have come to represent the city's innovation, community development, and economic progress in the Dover corporate environment. These businesses have not only made large financial contributions to Dover, but they have also defined the city's identity as a community and as a commercial centre.

Dover Downs Hotel & Casino, a legendary name in Delaware's gambling, hospitality, and entertainment industries, is one of the well-known names on the list. Dover Downs was initially established in 1969 as a horse racing track, but it has since grown to include a hotel, a casino, and a convention center. Due to its many businesses, it is now both a significant local employer and a popular tourist destination. Beyond the draw of the opulent suites and the glitz of the slot machines, Dover Downs has been a prominent supporter of community and educational initiatives in the area.

Playtex, the firm that created the modern bra and other latex clothing, was founded in Dover, revolutionizing women's clothing in the process. Playtex, which was established in the 1930s, had a huge influence on the regional economy as well as the larger cultural dialogue around women's fashion and personal care. The history of Playtex is intricately entwined with Dover's social development, reflecting over time-changing expectations and standards. Even though the business has expanded to become a recognized global brand, Dover residents are nonetheless proud of the company's roots there.

Summit Aviation is a leader in the fields of aviation and aerospace. Summit Aviation is a business with a variety of services, including government and military contracts and aircraft repair, and is situated at the Delaware Airpark close to Dover. Its significance has gone far beyond commercial to encompass significant contributions to public services and national defense. Dover is now a prominent player in the aerospace sector thanks to the existence of Summit Aviation, which has attracted expertise and resources that have improved the city's technological status.

Bayhealth Medical Center is a key institution in Dover for persons interested in the medical field. Bayhealth is more than just a hospital; as the primary healthcare provider in the area, it offers a vast network of programs for community outreach, research, and medical care. As it continues to adapt to meet the healthcare demands of a population that is expanding and becoming more diverse, the institution's progress over the years has matched Dover's own expansion.

Dover Mall is a major player in the retail and consumer services industries. Since it first opened in 1982, the mall has established itself as a major gathering place for locals and visitors alike for dining, shopping, and socializing. During the holiday season, when it transforms into a bustling marketplace and generates a sizable amount of sales tax money for the city, its economic significance is highlighted.

However, not all influential businesses are significant, well-known organizations. Dover has seen the emergence of many small firms and startups, particularly in the tech industry, which has helped to create a thriving entrepreneurial ecosystem. Even though these smaller businesses may not be as well-known as the bigger giants, they still play a big part in innovation and employment development.

It becomes apparent that the significant businesses that have shaped Dover's economic and social scene represent more than just financial data or job counts. These groups contribute to the overall identity of Dover, influencing its past, present, and unavoidably, its future. The rich tapestry that is Dover's ongoing tale is woven from the history, challenges, and victories of each enterprise.

Chapter 29: Visual Art and Movements in Dover

The contributions of the city to visual art frequently occupy a fascinating but perhaps underappreciated niche while examining the multifaceted fabric of Dover's history. Dover has been a quiet furnace of artistic endeavor, innovation, and expression despite not often being hailed as a national focus for cultural movements. The city's vibrant art culture is a reflection of its long history, diversified population, and continual engagement with more general cultural and aesthetic ideals.

Although Dover may not be able to lay claim to such legendary personalities, it has developed its own lively art culture that ranges from the traditional to the avant-garde. Delaware itself has been home to notable artists such as Howard Pyle, the father of American illustration. Dover has fostered a wide variety of artistic expressions, ranging from paintings and sketches inspired by the serene Delaware vistas to contemporary art installations that question traditional thought.

In particular, the city's projects for public art reflect this diversity. The cityscape of Dover is brightened with murals that adorn the sides of buildings and reflect historical occasions and everyday life. The city is made more beautiful, its history is remembered, and a public gallery that is open to all is created by these murals. As people of the community frequently assist in the creation and interpretation of these works, the inclusive aspect of this public art reflects Dover's communal culture and slightly blurs the distinction between artist and observer.

The city's aspirations for art are further reflected in Dover's art museums and galleries. A major collection of works made in Delaware can be found in venues like the Biggs Museum of American Art, which provides a cross-sectional picture of American artistic achievement. These organizations house a variety of artwork, from early American furniture and silver to contemporary works with a Delaware theme. These places serve as cultural archives as well as gathering places where people from various backgrounds can come together to appreciate and discuss art.

Another center for artistic interchange is the Arts Center/Gallery at Delaware State University, which specializes in experimental and modern art. The displays frequently engage in a creative discussion between local and national artists while examining complicated social topics including race, gender, and identity. The academic environment that is fostered by universities allows for the study, discussion, and appreciation of art by both students and outsiders.

Dover has also had a number of art festivals and fairs throughout the years that draw artists from all over the area. These gatherings are more than just for-profit endeavors; they serve to highlight the democratic nature of artistic creation. The festivals showcase the diversity of Dover's artistic life, whether it is a regional artist showcasing intricate paintings or a well-known local craftsperson selling their handmade wares.

Dover's artistic endeavors frequently cross paths with other forms of cultural expression and neighborhood initiatives. To provide multidisciplinary events and educational initiatives, the art scene works in conjunction with regional musicians, theater companies, and schools. This holistic strategy expands the influence and impact of art, turning it into a shared activity that improves the quality of life for people living in Dover.

Dover's dedication to fostering and presenting art remains a crucial component of its character as it develops. Although the local art scene may not garner much attention on a global scale, it has a significant impact on the neighborhood. The artwork of the city expresses its aspirations, reflects its diversity, and recounts its tales. It is a dynamic, living thing that actively contributes to Dover's ongoing story as well as reflecting its history and culture.

Chapter 30: Music and Musical Movements in Dover

The complex and multi-layered tapestry of Dover's musical legacy is too compelling to ignore when discussing the city's cultural development. The music scene in Dover is a vibrant fusion of tradition and contemporary, characterized by the confluence of various genres, cultures, and historical eras. The city's musical scene acts as a mirror reflecting its many cultures and their shared history, from the solemn hymns resonating in centuries-old churches to the throbbing beats of modern music festivals.

Like its visual arts, Dover's music is influenced by the stories that have shaped both the city and the state of Delaware as a whole. Since the city's establishment, hymns and spiritual songs have been an essential part of church services, giving sacred music a lengthy history. Religious music's ability to raise people's spirits and act as a symbol of the group's common values and beliefs. It provided a kind of refuge—a spiritual continuity in the face of change—whether that change was brought on by the Revolutionary War's upheaval, the Civil War's sociopolitical changes, or subsequent decades' cultural upheavals.

The city's musical preferences changed as it expanded and developed. Jazz, Blues, and Swing were increasingly popular in the early 20th century as a result of the Great Migration of African Americans from the South. Dover developed become a minor node in a broader cultural network that linked it to cities like New Orleans, Chicago, and New York. Jazz and blues contributed another layer to Dover's multicultural fabric by offering not just entertainment but also an expression of the African American experience. Concerts and lectures honoring these rich traditions were frequently held at Delaware State University, which was historically an African American institution of higher learning.

The Dover music scene underwent a period of variety and innovation in the middle to late 20th century. Rock 'n' Roll, Folk, and subsequently Punk and Hip-Hop, began to acquire popularity during this time. Local venues acted as crucibles for musical innovation, ranging from concert halls to temporary stages in basements and garages. Music evolved to become more than just a pastime in keeping with the times; it served as a platform for social and political expression. The youth's concerns, aspirations, and rebellions during this time period were mirrored in the music, whether they were against war, for civil rights, or just to challenge social conventions.

The Firefly Music Festival, which debuted in 2012, marked the zenith of this musical democratization. This festival, which is held every year at the Dover International Speedway, turned Dover into a musical hotspot and attracted a variety of talent, from independent bands to well-known performers from around the world. The festival has done more than just put Dover on the map for modern music; it has also provided a place where audiences from many genres can come together. Every year, for a few days, the festival transforms Dover into a microcosm of world musical styles, a place where electronic beats coexist with acoustic strums and where rap lyrics mix with classic rock chords.

The musical environment of Dover includes a sizeable portion devoted to music instruction. Instruction in a variety of musical disciplines, from classical to modern, is offered at schools, community centers, and specialized music institutions. These organizations act as both cradles for aspiring artists and centers for local participation in music on a grass-roots level. The younger generation develops an awareness for the cultural wealth that music reflects through participation in school choirs or through learning an instrument.

We learn that the different musical genres, venues, and festivals in Dover are interrelated threads in a larger cultural narrative as we travel through the city's musical past. Every note and lyric contribute to the city's changing identity, making music more than just a means of artistic expression but also a fundamental element of communal life. Both historical and contemporary music in Dover serves as a prism through which we can examine larger societal changes, such as changes in the population makeup, political upheavals, or changes in the general mood. It is a live, breathing feature of the city that is always changing and is always being influenced by the residents of Dover.

Chapter 31: Other Cultural Festivals in Dover

Dover's festivals are when the city's pulsating cultural heart beats the loudest since that is when customs from all over the world come together to create a colorful tapestry of experiences. These festivals serve as social processes that knit the city's cultural fabric together and transform Dover into a hub of interethnic conversation and enjoyment, making them more than merely local affairs. These occasions, whether commemorating Dover Days to respect the city's past or congregating for more recent additions like foreign cuisine festivals, serve as a common hearth where Dover residents may discuss their differences and the human experience as a whole.

The Dover Days Festival is one of the most established and enduring of these. This yearly event has a long history and is very connected to the identity of the city. The event, a festive mash-up of parades, colonial craft demonstrations, and reenactments, pays respect to Dover's heritage and attempts to capture the feel of the past. It acts as a platform for the next generation to connect with their past and encourages a sense of continuity that grounds the neighborhood in its historical setting.

However, local or historical topics are by no means the only ones covered by Dover's cultural events. The list of festivals has expanded along with the city's growth and diversification, reflecting the world community more and more. For instance, Dover now hosts the Caribbean Carnival, which enlivens the city's streets with the vibrant costumes, spirited dances, and rhythmic music of the region. Dancers in elaborate costumes parade down the streets during the festival, enticing onlookers into a celebration that crosses national and cultural barriers. The Caribbean community in Dover is able to invite people to share in their cultural feast while also displaying their background with pride.

Food festivals with international cuisines have developed into a gastronomic haven for Doverites in recent years. These events offer visitors a gourmet global tour, featuring everything from spicily spiced curries to delicate pastries. They serve as a subtle but savory method for many communities to contribute a piece of themselves and are a tribute to the cultural diversity that enhances Dover's identity. Prejudices dwindle as individuals from all walks of life come together to experience cuisine from around the world, and connections are found over shared plates and conversations. These festivals promote community relationships and intercultural understanding in addition to being a treat for the taste sensations.

It's not unusual to see festivals in Dover that highlight cultures from distant lands as the world becomes more interconnected. Asian cultural festivals, which are frequently put on by regional Asian American organizations, are an illustration of the expanding impact of Asian cultures in Dover. They offer a thorough and nuanced portrayal of Asia's different cultures by showcasing traditional music, dance, and art from several Asian nations. Similar to this, the African Heritage Festival showcases a fusion of traditional and modern art, music, and cuisine to honor the culture and contributions of African and African American communities.

These festivals serve as the yearly installments of Dover's continuing cultural narrative rather than only being one-time occurrences. They give the community opportunity for happiness, education, and cohesion while providing a break from the routine. Dover strengthens a sense of community by embracing a wide range of cultures and life experiences, emphasizing that the city's vitality lies in its diversity. These events act as touchstones, regularly recalibrating the city's feeling of community and serving to remind locals that, although coming from different backgrounds, they are all interwoven into the fabric of Dover. Therefore, cultural festivals in Dover serve as important tools for creating community cohesion and sustaining the inclusive spirit that best characterizes the city. They go beyond simply enhancing the city's social life.

Chapter 32: Key Educational Institutions

Educational institutions frequently stand out as pillars of greatness, knowledge, and societal advancement when one considers the foundation of any thriving community. These institutions have a particularly significant impact on the social and economic landscape as well as the intellectual character of Dover, Delaware. Public and private schools, colleges, and specialized institutes make up the city's educational landscape, and each one adds something particular to the city's intellectual capital and involvement in the community.

Delaware State University (DSU), a school with a rich history and heritage, is at the center of Dover's higher education system. DSU is one of the nation's historically black colleges and universities (HBCUs), having been established in 1891. The university has evolved through time from a tiny, predominately black institution to a diversified, all-encompassing institution. It serves as a hub for academic and cultural activities for a wide range of local, national, and international communities in addition to African American students. The university is renowned for its research initiatives in topics including neuroscience, optics, and agriculture. These programs frequently collaborate with other research institutions to develop a variety of fields. In keeping with its greater dedication to societal progress, it has also served as a breeding ground for community action and civil rights groups.

Dover's K–12 educational system is made up of a variety of public, private, and charter schools, each of which presents its own special opportunities and difficulties. The Capital School District, which is the main public school system, has long been a pillar of the neighborhood. This school system, which continuously modifies its curriculum and extracurricular activities to match the changing demands of the 21st century, has produced many of Dover's most notable individuals. The emphasis has switched in recent years to STEM (Science, Technology, Engineering, and Mathematics) education, educating pupils for a world that is driven by technology and is undergoing rapid change.

Alternative learning settings are provided by private schools like Holy Cross School and St. John's Lutheran School, which frequently incorporate religious and ethical principles into their curricula. These schools draw families looking for a more individualized education that is in line with their moral and spiritual principles. Despite being smaller in scale, these organizations play a significant role in helping kids cultivate a strong sense of community and personal responsibility—qualities that will serve them well as adults.

Dover is home to a number of vocational and specialty training institutions in addition to conventional educational courses. These include the Delaware Technical Community College, which provides two-year degrees and certifications in a range of subjects, and the Paul M. Hodgson Vocational Technical High School. These schools are designed for students who want to start working right away or who want to learn particular skills that don't necessarily require a four-year degree. It is impossible to emphasize the significance of these institutions for Dover's educational ecology; they close significant skills gaps in the job market and offer many locals realistic avenues for achieving financial stability.

Like the Dover Public Library, community learning centers and libraries offer as additional educational spaces by frequently hosting seminars, conferences, and community classes that address a variety of topics, from computer literacy to local history. These institutions are essential to lifelong learning because they make education available to people of all ages.

The common commitment to developing an educational environment that is centered on the entire development of the individual as well as one that is conducive to academic accomplishment binds these various threads together. Dover's educational institutions represent the city's diverse and multifaceted personality, whether it is through a public high school that offers robotics extracurriculars, a university that inspires social activity, or a vocational school that trains students for particular crafts. Each one serves as a learning environment for many facets of Dover life, from the intellectual and technological to the cultural and ethical. Through their work, these institutions shape the leaders, citizens, and innovators of the future who will continue to enhance Dover and, consequently, the larger fabric of American society.

Chapter 33: Dover's Role in Academia and Research

Dover may not have the same academic reputation as cities like Boston or the Silicon Valley, but it has gradually established a unique position in academics and research, making significant and quantifiable contributions to knowledge and innovation. Both the institutions that call Dover home and the local community are reflected in the city's interest in academia and research. Dover has become a more significant actor in numerous disciplines of academic study and applied research thanks to its distinctive fusion of historical solemnity and forward-looking optimism.

Delaware State University (DSU), which has shown a growing presence in fields like agricultural science, neuroscience, and renewable energy research, is a key contributor to Dover's academic achievements. DSU conducts cutting-edge studies through its research institutes and academic divisions that not only add to the body of scholarly literature but also provide practical applications. For instance, the university's agriculture department is vital to research into sustainable farming methods, which is significant for Delaware's farming community and beyond. DSU's contributions improve the worldwide conversation on sustainable agriculture through improving crop rotations, investigating organic farming techniques, and making the most use of available resources.

This type of research has tangible repercussions. They connect with regional farmers, decision-makers, and foreign academics, making Dover a key hub in this particular academic network. It's a potent illustration of how a city may shape debates and behaviors on a much bigger scale than its physical location or population would imply through the impact of its intellectual institutions.

The study of the healthcare industry, a crucial component of Dover's economy and a subject of growing academic interest, should not be disregarded. Clinical trials and studies on healthcare administration are only a few of the research projects in the city's hospitals and healthcare institutions that strive to enhance patient outcomes. These frequently involve nationwide partnerships or get funding from government grants, further integrating Dover into a wider academic network. It gives local medical practitioners a chance to use cutting-edge techniques and tools, guaranteeing that the standard of treatment is maintained and keeps rising.

Additionally, Dover has become a center for research into aerospace and national defense thanks to its advantageous location close to military installations like Dover Air Force Base. This spans a wide range, from logistical studies that seek to improve resource allocation to more specialized research targeted at cybersecurity and aerospace engineering. Thus, the military presence expands the academic and research environment in Dover by connecting it to government organizations and defense contractors that are eager to use regional findings for more general applications.

Another area where Dover excels is community-based research. For researchers interested in American history, social justice, and community development, the city is a great case study because of its extensive past and cultural diversity. Local historians and social scientists frequently examine the city's demographics and archives to learn more about a variety of subjects, including the effects of desegregation, the development of local government, and the history of distinct cultural communities in Dover. Their work frequently appears in academic publications, policy papers, and community outreach initiatives, further enhancing the city's intellectual life.

Finally, it's critical to recognize how smaller universities, vocational schools, and even K–12 educational institutions contribute to the development of an environment that values research and innovation. These ostensibly tiny contributions—whether they come from a high school science fair idea that goes viral or a community college program that turns into a startup—are the foundation of a vibrant academic environment.

By providing resources, human capital, and a supportive environment, the city supports these academic endeavors in a symbiotic connection, and in exchange, the academic labor's fruits contribute to the growth and renown of the city. Over time, this synergy strengthens Dover's developing reputation as a regional center for research and academics, elevating the city above its status as a mere blip on the academic map. Instead, Dover is evolving into a fascinating illustration of how concentrated academic and scientific activities may have an impact well beyond a city's boundaries, enlightening the rest of the globe with information, answers, and opportunities for a better future.

Chapter 34: Natural Disasters in Dover and their Impact

While tragic, natural catastrophes serve as turning points in the history of any area, providing a prism through which we can analyze a community's vulnerabilities and resiliency. Dover is not completely protected from the fury of nature, despite its geographically sheltered location. Over the years, the city has seen a variety of natural disasters, including as hurricanes, violent thunderstorms, and sporadic flooding. Each of these incidents has permanently altered Dover, altering not just its physical terrain but also its social structure, its system of government, and even how it approaches urban planning and crisis management.

Dover has experienced several particularly remarkable effects from hurricanes and tropical storms. These storms, which typically move along the Atlantic coast, have pummeled the city with heavy rainfall and violent gusts. Compared to coastal towns, Dover is somewhat protected from the full force of these storms, although the effects can still be significant. Roads flood, power lines collapse, and houses sustain damage. These storms are famous for their indiscriminate character; they affect both wealthy and impoverished communities equally, frequently revealing the disparities in infrastructure quality and disaster preparedness between various parts of the city.

The effects of severe storms on Dover go beyond only the immediate aftermath. For the community and its leaders, the path to recovery and restoration frequently provides an opportunity for reflection. Land usage, building regulations, and even social equity issues are raised. Hurricanes, for instance, have prompted extensive upgrades to drainage systems, revisions to building codes to make structures more wind-resistant, and the creation of more efficient disaster response plans. These reforms frequently go beyond simple policy changes. They stimulate local debates and scholarly research while encouraging a culture of readiness and adaptability.

Although less frequent, severe thunderstorms and tornadoes have also influenced Dover's perception of natural disasters. These circumstances, which are frequently unforeseen and transient, provide unique difficulties. The rapid onset gives little time for preparation, and while the damage is frequently highly limited and less extensive than that from hurricanes, it nonetheless causes major disruption in the impacted communities. Once more, the city's response extends beyond simple restoration. Such storm trends are examined in an effort to determine if they are isolated occurrences or a sign of more significant climate changes. These events are also opportunities for local government, in partnership with meteorologists and climate scientists, to improve emergency response methods, with a particular emphasis on speedy resource deployment and efficient communication techniques.

Flooding along the St. Jones River has also consistently been a problem, particularly since variable weather patterns are being brought on by climate change. Flooding incidents act as depressing reminders of the environmental weaknesses built into Dover's topography. Conversations regarding responsible land use and urban planning have frequently resulted from these events. Long-term planning discussions in the city are increasingly focused on issues like how close to develop to the river, how to manage runoff properly, and how to build structures that are resilient to flooding.

Additionally, each of these catastrophes offers a chance for intercommunity cooperation. As people band together to repair and recover, social barriers often dissolve as a result of natural disasters, if only momentarily. Local businesses provide free services or goods to people affected, neighborhoods organize cleanup crews, and a sense of communal spirit is frequently present. In a sense, the city's ability to persevere in the face of difficulty comes to define it.

Natural catastrophes have an even greater effect on Dover than the obvious damage they cause to the environment. These occurrences operate as impetuses for reflection, change, and civic engagement. They become a part of the city's communal memory, affecting community relations, urban planning, government, and personal behavior. The way Dover has handled natural disasters throughout the course of its lengthy history is evidence of the city's fortitude, adaptability, and unwavering dedication to protecting its citizens from nature's unpredictable wrath.

Chapter 35: History of Sports and Athletes from Dover

The history of athletics in Dover is more than simply a footnote or tangential aside; it is a dramatic story of triumph and camaraderie. Similar to how the city has seen periods of expansion, contraction, and resurrection, so has its sporting culture, which has been sustained by an eternal passion for physical competition. This passion has evolved through the years in a number of sports, including baseball, football, basketball, and even motorsports, and has given rise to local heroes, historical occasions, and cherished memories that have become essential to the character of the city.

Baseball is a sport that has some ties to Dover's early athletic heritage. Local teams started forming as early as the late 19th century, and games were frequently important communal social events. These weren't just fun activities; they were cultural occasions that drew sizable crowds and sparked a strong sense of community pride. The sport provided a venue for young men in the neighborhood to show their talent and sportsmanship while also giving neighborhood rivalries a place to play out in a cordial yet competitive setting. Even though Dover never had a Major League team, the city's affection for baseball has persisted over the years as it transitioned from amateur leagues to more structured systems.

The sporting scene in Dover has seen substantial growth for basketball as well. Particularly high school basketball games have been significant social events, frequently acting as a spark for neighborhood involvement. A city's attention has occasionally been drawn to local high schools' exploits during state finals, energizing residents to support their young athletes and forging hometown heroes in the process. Basketball courts have also served as testing grounds for talent, with some players later enjoying fruitful university or even professional careers.

Then there is the field of motorsports, which has had a tremendous uptick because to the Dover International Speedway, also referred to as the "Monster Mile." Since its opening in 1969, the speedway has played host to several NASCAR races, drawing spectators and competitors from all across the country. For many locals, Dover's modern character is connected with the scream of engines and the rush of high-speed competition. The speedway not only offers heart-pounding action, but it also serves as a significant economic driver for the city, drawing tens of thousands of tourists and bringing in big bucks for small businesses.

Dover has also served as a home for less popular sports in addition to these widely watched ones. The range of sports and the levels at which they are played is astonishing, from youth soccer leagues that have developed a new generation of football players to local golf courses that have hosted state championships to the increasing community of runners competing in marathons and charity runs. Even water sports have grown in popularity, with neighborhood swimming events drawing larger and more competitive crowds.

Dover's sports have frequently reflected greater cultural shifts. The desegregation of sports teams, the rise of female athletes, and the diversification of the most popular sports are all themes that have been visible in Dover's sports culture. In Dover, for instance, women's sports have increased significantly at the school and collegiate levels as a result of Title IX, which forbade sex-based discrimination in federally funded educational programs and activities. This has allowed young women to pursue athletic excellence in ways that were not possible for earlier generations.

This is a story of how sports have molded community identity, dismantled social barriers, and provided a forum for both individual and group expression, not merely a history of games played and victories. Sports in Dover are a microcosm of the city itself—dynamic, diverse, and ever-evolving. Whether it's a Little League coach teaching a group of children life lessons, a local athlete setting records and making it to the professional leagues, or a community coming together to support their home team in a state championship. The essence of a town that appreciates competition but values sportsmanship, strives for greatness but enjoys the journey, and may be deeply established in history but is never hesitant to accept change is captured in them, giving us a deeper view of the social fabric of Dover.

Chapter 36: Noteworthy Recreational Spaces

Recreational areas in Dover are more than just isolated green spaces or play areas dotted around an urban environment; they are lively stages on which the drama of neighborhood life plays out. Every park, every path, and every coastal area has a unique tale to tell—a story of people coming together and going it alone, of nature and culture, of the past and the present. Children take their first fumbling steps in these places, couples escape the world for a quiet moment, elderly people find comfort on a favorite old bench, and communities join together to celebrate, grieve, or just be.

Consider Silver Lake Park, a green haven tucked away close to the city's center. This park, which is well-known for its lovely lake and walking pathways, offers more than simply a peaceful haven. It serves as a dynamic portrait of Dover's diverse people. On any given day, you can come across joggers jogging alongside elderly people taking it easy, families having picnics by the lake, or amateur photographers taking pictures of the park's natural beauty. In addition to hosting community events like environmental awareness seminars and summer concerts, Silver Lake Park is a multipurpose recreational hub that nourishes both the body and the spirit.

The Delaware Agricultural Museum and Village is another interesting recreational area, despite not being a standard "park." Here, history is the main draw, and the museum offers a trip through time that takes visitors from Delaware's agricultural origins to the intricacies of contemporary farming. Families may discover the history of agriculture in Delaware at this hybrid recreational-educational location while taking their time browsing the inside and outdoor displays. It is both a nostalgic exercise and an eye-opener for the younger generation, who are not used to considering farming to be fundamental to their state's character.

Another gem among Dover's leisure areas is Schutte Park. It is a sanctuary for sports fans and is renowned for its numerous athletic facilities. The park's basketball courts, baseball and softball diamonds, and other features provide locals with a range of opportunities for physical recreation. The park transforms into a center of neighborhood sports on the weekends when neighborhood leagues take to the fields and spectators cheer them on. Beyond its sporting amenities, Schutte Park also has picnic spots and playgrounds, giving people who prefer a more sedate sort of amusement alternatives.

The St. Jones River Greenway, a celebration of the natural splendor that envelops Dover, should not be overlooked. The greenway has routes that meander through marshes and forests, making them great places to go birdwatching, take pictures, or just to relax. More than that, the Greenway makes a statement about the environment by preserving important habitats and providing information about regional ecosystems. It acts as a constant reminder of the need to keep natural preservation and urban growth in check.

Another example of this is the Fork Branch Nature Preserve, which offers a forested expanse where one may escape the bustle of the city without leaving its boundaries. Its trails take guests through a collection of native flora that serve as a reminder of how Delaware's landscapes seemed before development. The preserve is a representation of conservation efforts and provides a venue for environmental education; it frequently hosts school outings and led tours that concentrate on local flora and wildlife.

Additionally, Dover's recreational areas have historically been subtly political. Parks have served as the location for vigils, celebrations, and protests. They have observed the ebb and flow of social movements, watched the shifting demographics of Dover play out on their property, and stood as mute spectators to history being made. These areas, for instance, frequently served as the scene of conflicts over segregation and social justice throughout the civil rights era. They have recently hosted events in support of many social justice causes.

Therefore, when we talk about Dover's recreational areas, we're not just referring to their physical location. These serve as the city's heart, lungs, and soul. They are intersections where, if only briefly, people from many walks of life meet paths. They are time capsules that have encapsulated the spirit of each age in which they have lived. Perhaps most significantly, they serve as blank slates on which each generation imprints its unique characteristics, changing and redefining these areas as part of an ongoing conversation between the city and its inhabitants.

Chapter 37: Noteworthy Nature in Dover

The first things that come to mind when someone mentions Dover may be governmental structures, famous landmarks, or busy cities. However, woven throughout this fabric of human achievement and history is a narrative about nature that is equally rich, bright, and compelling in and of itself. In addition to being aesthetically pleasing, Dover's natural surroundings serve as a living example of the region's ecological richness and its nuanced interactions with human settlements.

The wetlands are the unsung heroes of natural Dover, so let's start there. These places, which are sometimes disregarded or even referred to as merely "swamps," are in fact crucial ecological hotspots. Wetlands such as the Little Creek Wildlife Area and the Ted Harvey Conservation Area serve as cradles for marine life, filters for pollutants, and flood-resistant natural barriers. Additionally, these habitats have a diverse range of species, including amphibians, crabs, and migratory birds like the American Black Duck. The wetlands provide a microcosm of ecological interactions and act as environmental health indicators for both scientists and nature lovers.

In terms of ecological significance, the wetlands may take center stage, but Dover's forests provide a calmer, more introspective sort of natural beauty. With their tree-lined walks and the peaceful rustle of leaves as the only background music, forested regions like Brecknock Park offer a pleasant getaway from city life. But these places are more than just pretty places.

They serve as living laboratories for biologists and botanists because they are home to a wide array of animal and plant species. For instance, Brecknock Park features meadows, freshwater ponds, hardwood and pine forests, all of which have their own distinct flora and fauna. Red foxes can be seen sneakily moving through the vegetation, hawks flying above, and turtles lazing by the ponds.

Waterbodies in Dover give yet another dimension to this biological tale, which is largely defined by woods and marshes. In addition to being a physical landmark, the St. Jones River is an essential component of the neighborhood ecosystem. The river serves as a hub for both recreational fishing and academic study because it is home to fish species including the Eastern mudminnow and the American shad. It acts as a real-world school where teachers and students may learn about everything from fish biology to water quality. The St. Jones River has been an essential economic resource for Dover throughout its history, supporting industries like shipbuilding and milling in addition to its scientific and recreational value.

The natural expanses of Dover are dynamic landscapes that experience seasonal and long-term changes rather than being static features to be passively admired. The first spring blossoms, the shifting colors of the fall leaves, and the bird migrations are all occurrences that immediately and visibly signal the passing of time. They serve as a reminder to Dover residents that the natural cycles never stop, no matter how much the city changes.

These natural areas, however, are dynamic; they too have histories and futures that are closely related to human activity. Successful and unsuccessful conservation efforts have left their imprint on the environment. The city is responding to the realization that the wellbeing of its natural areas is entwined with the wellbeing of its human population by placing an increasing emphasis on sustainable development. For instance, recent programs have sought to improve water quality, expand green spaces within the city, and restore natural habitats. These activities highlight the growing realization that Dover's natural beauty is a gift that needs deliberate stewardship rather than being a given.

In conclusion, Dover's notable natural features are an essential component of its character and provide a balance to its human-centric stories. Not only is it the setting in which human actions take place, but it also contributes to the local landscape in a dynamic and participatory way. The beauty and complexity of the ecosystems that surround us, as well as the ways in which we as a community interact with, depend upon, and alter our environment, are just a few of the things that the natural world around Dover asks us to consider. Whether it's a peaceful stroll in the forest, an educational excursion to the marshes, or a quiet moment by the river, Dover's natural surroundings are more than simply picturesque backdrops; they are an integral part of the city's history.

Chapter 38: Environmental Issues in Dover

Dover's environmental story is a complicated one, rich with the interaction of the wonders of nature and the occasionally bleak reality of human effect. Dover, the state's capital, is faced with a number of environmental problems that are not simply regional but frequently even more worldwide in scope. As the city seeks to balance its development with sustainable practices, these concerns have significant economic, social, and political repercussions that call for thorough discussion and aggressive answers.

Pollution of the air and water has long been a problem for Dover. Runoff from urban regions and agricultural areas has degraded the St. Jones River, a crucial watercourse. Eutrophication is a result of nutrient pollution, primarily from nitrogen and phosphorus, which promotes algal blooms that deplete the water's oxygen content and render it unsuitable for many species. Given the river's significance for leisure activities like fishing and its role as a habitat for a variety of marine life, such water quality issues are particularly concerning. Stricter agricultural runoff rules and community awareness campaigns are only two examples of initiatives that have been put in place to improve water quality, but they are nevertheless a source of continuous concern and research.

Another issue that needs care is air quality. Despite not having as much industrialization as some other American cities, Dover's air pollution levels occasionally exceed the recommended limits for pollutants like ground-level ozone and particulate matter due to rising vehicular traffic, a lack of reliable public transportation, and proximity to industrial areas. This has an influence on public health as well as the environment, with the most severe effects on vulnerable groups including the elderly and children. The ongoing discussions about reducing air pollution include switching to cleaner energy sources and enhancing public transit.

The third and most important environmental issue is land usage. The necessity to protect natural habitats clashes with pressure to develop land for infrastructure, commercial space, and housing. Urban sprawl has an impact on the availability of green spaces as well as other issues, such as the loss of important ecosystems and a rise in car dependence. Sustainable development issues are taking center stage with each new development initiative. Environmental impact studies, which demand that developers take into account the long-term ecological effects of their projects, are increasingly influencing the discussion surrounding land use.

Another aspect that must be considered is environmental justice. Historically, environmental dangers, such as the placement of waste management facilities or exposure to contaminants, have disproportionately impacted low-income neighborhoods and minorities. Community organizers and officials have been working to eliminate these inequalities in recent years by incorporating environmental justice principles into planning and decision-making procedures.

Despite these difficulties, Dover has served as a hub for creative environmental solutions. Public-private partnerships have evolved to finance green activities, from waste management initiatives that encourage recycling and composting to tree-planting campaigns. Environmental education is being incorporated into school curricula as a subject of study as well as a lens through which to evaluate other academic disciplines including history, science, and social studies. Governmental agencies and grassroots organizations are collaborating to raise public knowledge of sustainable practices. These initiatives, while not without their growing pains, represent a shift from the mere awareness of problems to concrete remedies.

Furthermore, Dover plays a special role in determining Delaware's environmental regulations due to its status as the state capital. The laws that are passed here can serve as a benchmark for the state and, on occasion, even have an impact on larger national discussions. Dover could serve as a hub for sustainable innovation because the dialogue about environmental challenges there transcends local boundaries and sometimes even crosses state lines.

To sum up, Dover's environmental problems are complex and multidimensional, balancing economic viability, social equality, and ecological responsibility. They shape not only the natural landscape but also the human experience within the city since they are woven into the fabric of daily life and administration. They are issues that demand tangible answers based on scientific knowledge, widespread public awareness, and political will. They also come with ethical requirements and practical urgencies. They serve as a reminder that Dover's history is still being written and that the decisions we make today will have an impact on how the natural and human worlds in the city develop throughout time.

Chapter 39: Technological Advancements from Dover

Technology frequently acts as a narrative link between different eras in any account of a location's history, indicating changes in way of life, industry, and even thought. This pattern continues in Dover. Dover, a city that has played a crucial role in shaping American history, has not only adapted to new technologies but also given rise to some intriguing innovations. Technology has been a driving force of progress that has influenced Dover's economic, social, and even cultural fabric from its early years when windmills and basic machinery propelled its industries to the present day, defined by breakthroughs in telecommunications, transportation, and healthcare.

Let's go back to the early 20th century, when Dover started to become known for its leadership in agricultural innovation. Scientific farming methods were utilized to grow hardier crops and increase yields at experimental research farms in the region. In addition to revolutionizing local farming practices, these initiatives also influenced larger agricultural trends and paved the way for sustainable farming practices. These technological developments had a significant impact on a region that was primarily dependent on agriculture, not only increasing economic output but also reshaping the surrounding countryside.

Let's fast-forward to World War II, a time of widespread strife that called for tremendous technological improvement in a variety of fields. The Dover Army Airfield (now Dover Air Force Base), in Dover, became the scene of important technological advancements in logistics and aviation. The complex has served as a center for research and development in addition to being one of the biggest military cargo airports in the entire world. The innovation culture that the military presence has cultivated has contributed to breakthroughs in logistics software, aircraft repair technologies, and even medical fieldwork.

Dover entered the field of educational technology in the years following World War II, thanks in large part to the existence of institutions like Delaware State University. The university led the way in incorporating computer sciences into its curriculum in the 1960s and 1970s, years before many other universities. A workforce well-versed in technology has resulted from this emphasis on technology in education, but it has also aided in the creation of instructional software and online learning resources with wider uses.

It is impossible to talk about technological improvements in Dover without bringing up fintech, or finance technology. Numerous financial organizations have chosen Delaware as their corporate headquarters due to the state's favorable corporation rules. This has encouraged the development of a tech-savvy banking sector in Dover that has been at the forefront of creating fraud detection algorithms, safe digital transaction techniques, and customer support technology. These developments have benefited the local economy in addition to having a spillover influence on national and occasionally international fintech trends.

Dover has advanced in green technology as well, in part because to the pressing need for sustainable growth. The city's research facilities have developed advances in wastewater treatment that are intended to lessen the ecological impact of development. Despite being on a lower scale than in other states, solar and wind energy projects have gained speed thanks to both public and private financing. Sustainability has been a key component of Dover's growth narrative as city planners and developers adopt more energy-efficient technologies, from smart street lighting to electric public transit.

These technical advancements, which range from banking and green technology to agriculture and aeronautics, not only make for gripping individual stories but also provide a multi-layered perspective of the city's development and adaption across time. Technology in Dover is not a solitary industry but rather a network of innovations that connect, disturb, and transform several facets of city life. It illustrates the ambition, adaptability, and significance of the city in larger movements that go far beyond the boundaries of Dover or even Delaware. These developments are proof of human brilliance, and they also act as the foundation for upcoming discoveries. They make us ponder how technology will continue to influence Dover over the next few years, both in ways we can already see and in numerous more ways we can't even begin to fathom.

Chapter 40: The Future Outlook for Dover

In our examination of Dover's rich history, as we get closer to the present, it is more important than ever to look ahead. The capital city of Delaware is at an interesting crossroads where historical legacies and modern realities intersect to produce a dynamic roadmap for what lies ahead. This is due to its history of resilience, inventiveness, and flexibility. Even though forecasting the future is rife with uncertainties, some significant developments and continuing projects give us invaluable information about the potential courses that Dover may take in the years to come.

The question of sustainable development comes first. As we've seen, Dover faces immediate and serious environmental concerns that are neither insignificant nor far away. Due to the seriousness of these issues, a variety of solutions, including community engagement and legislative action, have been made in an effort to achieve long-term sustainability. Future trends in this area suggest that green technologies, renewable energy, and eco-friendly urban planning may receive more attention. Projects to conserve water and initiatives to enhance air quality could be incorporated into the city's development plans. Dover's position as the state capital also makes it a potential leader in environmental policymaking for Delaware and perhaps even a model for other small American cities as concerns about climate change become more heated.

Diversification seems to be the key to the future of the economy. Although industries like finance and agriculture are likely to remain important players, there is an increasing awareness of the need to diversify the city's economic foundation. Sectors with promise include technology, healthcare, and tourism. Dover has already shown its abilities in the field of fintech, which is supported by Delaware's welcoming business environment, and may continue to grow in this sector. The interaction of the business community with academic institutions like Delaware State University may promote an ecosystem of innovation and entrepreneurship, turning the city into a center for new businesses and scientific endeavors.

Dover's population is diversifying, and this variety may have a big impact on how the city develops its social and cultural fabric. The blending of many communities brings a range of viewpoints, enhancing the arts, gastronomy, and even political debate of the city. Dover must successfully juggle tradition and change as it becomes a more globally minded city. Events, festivals, and public areas will probably more clearly represent this cosmopolitan mentality.

Without a question, education will remain a pillar of Dover's future. With a young population and expanding educational resources, the city has a special chance to become a hub for intellectual success. The goal of on-going technological advancements and educational reforms is to get the next generation ready for the opportunities and difficulties of a world that is changing quickly. The educational institutions in the city might cooperate with businesses more frequently to provide practical, skill-based education alongside traditional academics, resulting in a workforce that is both adaptable and specialized.

Another issue that requires attention is the development of the infrastructure. Dover must upgrade its infrastructure while maintaining its environmental objectives in light of its expanding population and the requirement for sustainable practices. This infrastructure development may include smart city programs, which use technology to optimize everything from energy use to traffic flow.

Last but not least, Dover's governance will probably need to be more responsive and democratic than ever. Due to the complexity of current issues, inclusive decision-making that involves a variety of stakeholders is required, from common people and small businesses to academic institutions and non-profits. Due to this, community forums, public meetings, and partnerships between the local government and diverse industries may increase.

The guiding principles of sustainability, inclusion, innovation, and adaptation provide positive directions even though the specifics of Dover's future have yet to be written. Dover has the resources it needs to successfully traverse the intricacies of the 21st century given its rich history and the dynamism of its people. There is no doubt that Dover's story is far from done, and the chapters still to be written contain the promise of adventure, difficulty, and lasting significance. The future is not just a theoretical idea; it is a dynamic, living thing that is being formed by the decisions and deeds of its citizens. when a result, when we put this book to bed, we throw open the floodgates to a plethora of fresh tales that will shape Dover in the years and decades to come.

Chapter 41: Must-See Locations in Dover

Delaware State Capitol (Legislative Hall)	411 Legislative Ave, Dover, DE 19901	This iconic structure, which serves as the capital of Delaware, is both an architectural wonder and a cultural icon.
First State Heritage Park	121 Duke of York St, Dover, DE 19901	A large park honoring Delaware's past that includes the Old State House and other historical attractions.
Dover International Speedway	1131 N Dupont Hwy, Dover, DE 19901	This location, also referred to as the "Monster Mile," is a haven for NASCAR enthusiasts and hosts numerous other events.
Air Mobility Command Museum	1301 Heritage Rd, Dover AFB, DE 19902	An intriguing aviation museum that has a sizable collection of antique airplanes and military relics.
Johnson Victrola Museum	375 S New St, Dover, DE 19901	A lovely early 20th-century structure that serves as the home of a museum devoted to the history of sound recording.
Biggs Museum of American Art	406 Federal St, Dover, DE 19901	Includes a broad selection of American artwork from many eras, as well as furniture, silver, and fine arts.
Spence's Bazaar	550 S New St, Dover, DE 19904	A bustling neighborhood market with a wide selection of goods, including fresh produce and antiques.

Pickering Beach	Pickering Beach Rd, Dover, DE 19901	A calm beach location with a variety of bird species and horseshoe crab spawning.
Bombay Hook National Wildlife Refuge	2591 Whitehall Neck Rd, Smyrna, DE 19977	An important migratory bird refuge with walking paths and photo possibilities.
Delaware Agricultural Museum and Village	866 N Dupont Hwy, Dover, DE 19901	A celebration of Delaware's agricultural heritage featuring displays on farming methods, equipment, and rural living.

Don't miss out!

Visit the website below and you can sign up to receive emails whenever Henry Church publishes a new book. There's no charge and no obligation.

https://books2read.com/r/B-A-GDIAB-QHJOC

BOOKS 2 READ

Connecting independent readers to independent writers.

Also by Henry Church

American Cities History Guidebook Series
Charlottesville, Virginia: Historical Guide for Travelers
Williamsburg, Virginia: Historical Guide for Travelers
Richmond, Virginia: Historical Guide for Travelers
Norfolk & Virginia Beach: Historical Guide for Travelers
Winchester, Virginia: Historical Guide for Travelers
Baltimore, Maryland: Historical Guide for Travelers
Dover, Delaware: Historical Guide for Travelers
Arlington, Virginia: Historical Guide for Travelers

About the Publisher

Fiel LLC is dedicated to providing high-quality content at affordable prices, utilizing state-of-the-art processes and advanced content generation systems to ensure a superior reading experience. All books published by Fiel LLC are for entertainment purposes only. Fiel LLC authors use pen names and are not experts in any field, so no content should be taken as financial, medical, legal, or professional advice. All information provided is subject to change, and readers are encouraged to verify the latest details through their own research.

9 798822 387720